Twelve Vital Questions

Leith Samuel

W0009105

BRYNTIRION PRESS

© Leith Samuel 1969, 1998
First published in this form 1998
ISBN 1 85049 142 9

Cover design by Phil Boorman @ burgum boorman ltd

Published by **Bryntirion** Press
Bryntirion, Bridgend CF31 4DX, Wales, UK
Printed by Interprint Ltd., Malta

Contents

Preface

I would like to take this opportunity for saying 'Thank you' from the bottom of my heart to all those who have had anything to do with the material found in this slim volume, some chapters of which originally appeared in *Vital Questions* which Victory Press published in 1969.

Particularly I would like to express my appreciation to the Rev. David Kingdon who has superintended the final stages of the publication. Where the material fell short of today's demands he has with my full approval filled in the gaps.

The whole product would have been lost to the diminishing reading public but for the hard work of the Managing Editor of the Bryntirion Press at Bryntirion.

Leith Samuel
Frinton-on-Sea
June 1998

1
Where is final
authority to be found?

Sola scriptura is a Latin phrase meaning 'Scripture alone'. This phrase has been used since the sixteenth century to describe the principle that, in spiritual and religious matters, Scripture, the Holy Bible or God's written Word, and Scripture alone, is the final authority for Christian living and belief. Those who maintain this approach to Scripture acknowledge that there are other sources of information and indeed revelation in the world (see Romans 1:19-21; 2:14-16), but they reject these as not having supreme authority, insisting that they will not be bound to believe or practise any teaching which is inconsistent with the Bible.

Scripture alone

But why the Bible alone? Why not a combination of Scripture, reason and tradition as advocated in the 1994 Catechism of the Roman Catholic Church? Why not a combination of the Bible, the Koran, the Bhagavad Gita and all the other sacred writings looked on as 'Scripture' by the adherents of other faiths around the world? The answer is quite simple. The Bible alone is the Word of God, and it is God alone who is truth. The Westminster Confession of Faith states:

> The Authority of the Holy Scripture, for which it ought
> to be believed and obeyed, dependeth not upon the

testimony of any man or Church, but wholly upon God (who is truth itself), the author thereof; and therefore it is to be received, because it is the Word of God (chapter 1; section IV).

The Confession goes on to say:

The whole counsel of God, concerning all things necessary for his own glory, man's salvation, faith, and life, is either expressly set down in Scripture, or by good and necessary consequence may be deduced from Scripture: unto which nothing at any time is to be added, whether by new revelations of the Spirit, or traditions of men (chapter 1, section VI).

There are two portions of Scripture that mean much to those who totally accept *sola scriptura*. The first is 2 Peter 1:20,21—'Above all, you must understand that no prophecy of Scripture came about by the prophet's own interpretation. For prophecy never had its origin in the will of man, but men spoke from God as they were carried along by the Holy Spirit.' The second portion is 2 Timothy 3:16,17—'All Scripture is God-breathed and is useful for teaching, rebuking, correcting and training in righteousness, so that the man of God may be thoroughly equipped for every good work.'

'God-breathed' may sound feeble to some, but this is not the case. It is a translation of the single word *theopneustos*, which means that God has breathed out his own thoughts into the minds of the writers. The words expressing the thoughts of God come from God, even if they are words drawn from the vocabulary of the man penning them. The origin of Scripture, therefore, is not with man but with

God. This fact gives its words nothing less than divine authority. God's thoughts are not like today's news, ephemeral, fleeting, and soon passing; they are for ever settled in heaven. Psalm 119:89 states, 'Your word, O Lord, is eternal; it stands firm in the heavens. Your faithfulness continues through all generations; you established the earth, and it endures.' Matthew 24:35 says, 'Heaven and earth will pass away, but my words will never pass away.' Here is final authority indeed.

Although God gives to his church Bible teachers or leaders (by whatever name we may know them), it is clear that everything they say must be tested. Even the personal authority of Peter, one of Jesus' disciples, and an apostle and leader of the early Christian church, had to be subject to that revealed truth (Galatians 2:14). He must walk in the light, and so must we!

The apostle Paul's great yardstick was not to trust in good feelings but in great facts—the revealed facts of the gospel. Our final authority, then, is God speaking through his Word, the Bible. The right of private judgment belongs to every believer; we must take no man as our final authority, whether he be Roman priest, Indian guru or Protestant pastor. The all-important question is, What does the Bible say? Here the mind of God is revealed. In Britain we have the great advantage of having the Bible translated into our mother tongue. We do not have to know Hebrew or Greek to know what God is saying. Thank God for William Tyndale, the sixteenth-century Bible translator, and the long line of men who in Christ's name have sought to bring the basic Tyndale translation up to date! We need have no difficulty in understanding the meaning of the original inspired words, even though it is the working of the Holy Spirit alone that can make us realise the full significance of

11

the words and give us the strength to live in the light.

In his classic, *Early Christian Doctrines* (Adam & Charles Black, third edition), J. N. D. Kelly says, 'What Christianity inherited from Judaism is the conception of the divine inspiration of the Holy Scripture.' Whenever our Lord and his apostles quoted the Old Testament it is plain that they regarded it as the Word of God. Jerome, the early Christian scholar, stated that 'In the divine Scriptures every word, syllable, accent and point is packed with meaning.' Kelly was not known as an evangelical. However, he recognised that the early church believed in the inerrancy of Scripture when he stated,

> It goes without saying that the fathers envisaged the whole of the Bible as inspired. It was not a collection of disparate segments, some of divine origin and others of merely human fabrication . . . the general view of the fathers was that Scripture was not only exempt from error but it contained nothing that was superfluous.

God's Word is true

There are many references in Scripture to the God of the Bible being the God of truth. The Hebrew word *emunah* means steadfastness, stability, utter worthiness. A number of texts bring out this point very forcefully. Here is a selection of them:

> He is the Rock, his works are perfect,
>   and all his ways are just.
> A faithful God who does no wrong,
>   upright and just is he.
>   (Deuteronomy 32:4)

12

The LORD . . . comes to judge the earth.
He will judge the world in righteousness
    and the peoples in his truth.
>   (Psalm 96:13)

He has remembered his love
    and his faithfulness to the house of Israel.
>   (Psalm 98:3a)

For the LORD is good and his love
    endures for ever.
>   (Psalm 100:5)

Another Hebrew word, *emeth*, puts a slightly different emphasis on the meaning of truth. Here it means 'right, sure, trustworthy'. The Psalmist says in Psalm 43:3, 'Send forth your light and your truth, let them guide me.' God revealed himself to Moses on Mount Sinai as 'The LORD God, merciful and gracious, longsuffering, and abundant in goodness and truth' (Exodus 34:6 AV). Christians know that it is at the cross of Christ that 'Mercy and truth are met together; righteousness and peace have kissed each other' (Psalm 85:10 AV). The wonderful mercy of God, and the awful truth about us in all our sin and need, have met one another at the place called Calvary. The truth about God is that he is a God of righteousness who cannot turn a blind eye to sin, ours or anybody else's. The mercy of God is that he was prepared to send his Son to die the death due to us. This God of righteousness, mercy and truth is our final authority. But this authority is not brought home to us in a vacuum. It is mediated to us through 'the Book of Truth' (Daniel 10:21). What Scripture says, God says, that we may 'know the certainty of the words of truth . . .' (Proverbs 22:21 AV).

13

Jesus Christ: God's final authority

In the Old Testament section of the Bible, God spoke to his people Israel in many different ways. God revealed himself, his nature, and the truth about himself, through the prophets by way of dreams, visions, voices and angelic visitations. In the New Testament, however, we see that those means of revelation become less prominent following the greatest and fullest revelation of God, when God himself came to earth in the person of the Lord Jesus Christ. Jesus Christ came with the complete revelation of God, to which nothing may be added and from which nothing may be subtracted (Hebrews 1:1-2).

The Lord Jesus Christ came into the world to reveal the truth of God the Father. Indeed, because Jesus Christ is God the Son, he is himself called Truth. And because God's truth is eternal and unchangeable and consistent within itself, there are no contradictions between the partial revelations of the old dispensation and the complete revelation of the new. Christ came to do his Father's will, and all the words he spoke he received from his Father. In all things Jesus said he was under the authority of his Father.

There are many examples in Scripture of Christ showing us that he is under the authority of God. One of these is John 12:48-50 where Christ says,

> There is a judge for the one who rejects me and does not accept my words; that very word which I spoke will condemn him at the last day. For I did not speak of my own accord, but the Father who sent me commanded me what to say and how to say it. I know that his command leads to eternal life. So whatever I say is just what the Father has told me to say.

14

Christ referred to his Father in heaven as his final authority and accepted the Old Testament as being the revelation of his Father's will, strategy and detailed plans. He shared with his Father in the active illumination of the minds of the Old Testament prophets and the inspiration of their written words. He became servant of those written words in the days of his life on earth. 'You diligently study the Scriptures,' he said, 'because you think that by them you possess eternal life. These are the Scriptures that testify about me . . .' (John 5:39). In John 10:35 he says, 'The Scripture cannot be broken.' Like his seamless robe for which the soldiers gambled at his crucifixion, the Scriptures cannot be torn apart.

Christ only does what is in the Father's will

Because of the unity of truth, the Lord Jesus Christ does not act outside the dictates of Scripture; for what it says, God says. In Matthew 26:53-54 Christ states, 'Do you think I cannot call on my Father, and he will at once put at my disposal more than twelve legions of angels? But how then would the Scriptures be fulfilled that say it must happen in this way?' The reference to the angels is found in Psalm 103:20-21. But Christ knew that although the angels were ready to do his bidding it was not the right time for them to act, for they would be acting outside of Scripture. He had to go to the cross alone, and in a certain way, so that Scripture would be fulfilled. Isaiah 53:7 says, 'He was oppressed and afflicted, yet he did not open his mouth; he was led like a lamb to the slaughter, and as a sheep before her shearers is silent, so he did not open his mouth.' What God breathes out and what Scripture says, Christ does. They cannot be separated. Could there be a clearer indication of the authority he was under, or a stronger claim for

15

the divine inspiration and infallibility of the teaching he was giving?

The Lord's promises are for us

The Saviour promised his first disciples that when the Holy Spirit came upon them in power, he would guide them into all truth (John 16:13)—that is, all the truth about him we Christians would ever need to know. For the first disciples this promise meant inspiration. They wrote inspired words. For us it means illumination. We read inspired words with an understanding that would be quite beyond us but for the help and powerful working of the same Holy Spirit.

Do you call yourself a Christian? Then your mind as well as your spirit must be subjected to the Christ of the Scriptures. Our Lord's words of promise are recorded for us in John 7:16-17. 'My teaching is not my own. It comes from him who sent me. If anyone chooses to do God's will, he will find out whether my teaching comes from God or whether I speak on my own.' To the Jews who had believed in him Jesus said, 'If you hold to my teaching, you are really my disciples. Then you will know the truth, and the truth will set you free' (John 8:31-32). Free from guilt and the grip of sin, free from slavery to Satan, free from the fear of man, free from the fear of destruction, free from the fear of a wasted life—going from one awful mess to another. In John 17:17 our Lord prays for all those his Father has given to him. He says: 'Sanctify them by the truth; your word is truth.' In his great mercy God not only sets free those who put their trust in his Son but, through his words of truth, he delivers us from the power of darkness and makes us fit for his service. This is perfect freedom.

The Word of God is sufficient, for it supplies all I need to know about God and his Son, all I need to know about the

16

Holy Spirit and his gracious workings. This is the word by which the gospel was preached to us. This is the word by which God brought us to faith. James 1:18 states, 'He chose to give us birth through the word of truth, that we might be a kind of firstfruits of all he created.' This is the word which brought us into God's family and which makes us 'live' as Christians. This is the word we must be under, and must be seen to be under. God forbid that we should ever give the impression that we are over or above the Word of God. Here, and here alone, is our final authority. Scripture is all we need. In the hands of the original donor we must come to his Word; not simply to black print on white paper, but to the everlasting Word of the eternal God. O Lord, 'Open my eyes that I may see wonderful things in your law' (Psalm 119:18).

2
What is God's way
of salvation?

'A re you suggesting I'm not good enough to go to heaven
when I die? You must be joking! I've never done anybody any harm in all my life! I'm not a sinner like some
people I know. The newspapers are full of real sinners.
Please don't bracket me with them. I'm simply appalled at
some of the things people get up to these days. And I'm
certainly not a hypocrite like some people round here who
go to church regularly. Don't start suggesting that God will
keep me out of heaven just because I'm not a regular at
Holy Communion. I'm doing my best; and nobody can do
better than their best. God knows that and God is fair. He
won't expect me to do better than my best. I would agree
that I'm not as religious as some, but I'm just as sincere as
the average churchgoer. I reckon I've as good a chance as
most of getting into any heaven there may be!'

Our best not good enough
Perhaps the man who said this was unusually articulate.
Few of us could put it into such a sustained argument. But
a lot of nice people think this way. If you are one of them, it
may come as a bit of a shock to you to be told that the best
we can do will never qualify us for heaven, whether we are
regular churchgoers or only darken a church doorstep for
weddings, christenings and funerals. But we can never

qualify for salvation and heaven by doing our best. This is all part of what we may call 'the bad news about us'.

No matter how hard we try, whether after a birthday or in the wake of New Year resolutions, our most earnest efforts to live a really good life and to do good to others are marred by selfishness. It is natural for us to live a life revolving round ourselves rather than round what God wants us to do with our lives. Self-centredness is the essence of sin. All other sins spring from this root, and we were born with this root firmly implanted within us.

It does not matter how strong-minded we are or how charming other people find us, we are quite unable to make ourselves fit for God's presence. You know a garage is a place for a car. But a bicycle does not become a car by leaving it regularly in the garage. No more does a person become a Christian simply by regular attendance at a good church where the gospel of the Lord Jesus Christ is regularly preached. The maker's handbook, the Bible, makes it crystal clear that 'We all, like sheep, have gone astray, each of us has turned to his own way' (Isaiah 53:6). We have followed the devices and desires of our self-centred hearts. We desperately need a Saviour, someone to do for us what we cannot do for ourselves. The Bible says we are all the same, no matter how respectable or how much better than others we may think we are (and no matter who agrees with us!). We all fall short of God's standards. This means, among other things, that while some people may impress us by their kindness, helpful actions and generous gifts to charitable causes, they do not impress the living God enough for him to consider them worthy of everlasting life, worthy of heaven when they die.

Why not? The Bible makes it very clear that no one can possibly earn everlasting life. Everlasting life is a gift which only God can give, and he has put certain non-negotiable terms around this gift. 'For the wages of sin is death; but the gift of God is eternal life in Jesus Christ our Lord' (Romans 6:23). No Jesus Christ, no everlasting life with Christ; only the misery of an endless existence without him. The warm-hearted approval of our friends at the end of our fast-passing days will be no compensation for us if we find ourselves rejected by the God who is the final inescapable judge.

The English poet W. H. Henley wrote, 'I am the master of my fate, I am the captain of my soul.' Do you find these words somewhat arrogant or quite acceptable? They are certainly very contemporary. Self-determination and self-fulfilment are very popular ideas today. But the Bible makes it plain (Isaiah 53:6; Romans 3:23) that these ideas are far removed from those that please God. He is not only our maker but also our final judge.

Make no mistake about it, we are completely powerless to save ourselves from the sinfulness and selfishness that is to be found in all of us. We have known what was wrong and done it. We have known what was right and not done it. Instinctively we have put our own self-interest first. Others may come next if they are useful to us, and God comes last, if he actually comes into the equation at all. The best of us has failed to love God with all our heart and soul and mind and strength. Each of us is guilty of the greatest sin in the world, the breaking of the first and greatest commandment. We can neither clear our past nor change our hearts. Left to ourselves we shall die in our sins. What a bleak prospect!

God's good news

So much for the bad news about man: now for the good

news. The good news is centred in God's Son, the Lord Jesus Christ. Unlike us he chose his mother, his birthplace and his time of arrival. Unlike us he lived a perfect life on earth for some thirty-three years. He took from his mother all he needed for true humanity except sin. He knew no sin (2 Corinthians 5:21). In him was no sin (Hebrews 4:15). He is the only man without sin that the world has ever seen. On the first Good Friday he offered up his sinless life as a sin-offering which was sufficient to atone for the sin of a rebellious lost world. John Calvin, the sixteenth-century Reformer, wrote, 'The propitiation is as wide as the sin'— that is, sufficient to atone for the greatest sin, efficient for those who repent and believe, whatever their colour or race. He became a substitute for all his people. He paid the price of their sin. He took the blame as if he had committed all their sin himself. No wonder John the Baptist cried out, 'Look, the Lamb of God, who takes away the sin of the world!' (John 1:29).

Paid in full

Christ paid in full the price of sin. God is righteous as well as merciful. Sin had to be dealt with. John Wycliffe, who has been called the 'Morning Star of the Reformation', said: 'It was man that sinned and it was man that deserved to die. God became man so that he could suffer the death due to us and then hold out to us the great free gifts of full forgiveness and everlasting life.' The hands that hold these gifts before us are clean. God has not compromised his justice in the interests of his mercy. He who met in full the cost of forgiveness, by dying under the judgment due to sinners, rose from the dead. That first Easter Sunday he left his tomb outside the city wall of old Jerusalem empty apart from the grave-clothes. His resurrection is 'one of the best

21

attested facts of history'. In his booklet *Verdict on the Empty Tomb,* lawyer Val Grieve analyses the evidence and comes to the conclusion that it is very strong in favour of a factual resurrection. He looks at two types of evidence; the *direct* evidence of the disciples and those who saw Christ after his resurrection, together with the *real* evidence of Christ himself, who today lives in the lives of those he has saved. Christ tore history in two. Time is divided into BC (before Christ) and AD (Anno Domini; in the year of our Lord). All over the world the silent witness to this fact of Christ's resurrection is on the top of our newspapers. We date our birthdays from the calendar—he has dated the calendar from his birthday.

But what has the life, death and resurrection of Christ got to do with us? In our modern society the concept of sacrifice or blood-offering seems alien, even repulsive. Yet in many countries animal sacrifice continues to be a major part of ceremonial religion. The practice of animal sacrifice in the Old Testament Jewish religion sheds light on the purpose of Christ's death. Under the law laid down by God in the Old Testament, long before Jesus Christ came down to earth, a Jew who had done something wrong was obliged to bring a sin-offering, usually an animal. But he did not just bring his sin-offering and leave the priest to do everything for him. He had to lay his hand on the head of his animal substitute. The innocent animal died in his place. The laying on of hands was a visible way of identifying with his substitute. The guilty man confessed that he deserved to die, but because of God's arrangement the innocent animal died in his place. God's justice was satisfied. Not that the animal could take away his sin, but it pointed to the one whose death alone could take away sin. The animal sacrifice could cover sin; only the death of the Son of God could take it

22

away. But faith in the substitute's death was accounted by God as faith in his Son, not yet born.

When the repentant Jew laid his hands on his substitute and confessed his sins over its innocent head, the animal was slain instead of him, the guilty sinner. God's justice was satisfied by the substitutionary sacrifice and God's mercy was found by the sinner. He could then join in the temple worship without fear of disqualification. Now had this Old Testament Jew been able to read the letter to the Hebrews in the New Testament, he would have gained a perfect understanding of what had taken place. The symbol has given place to the reality. The Lamb of God has been slain. Whereas animal sacrifices could provide a cover for sins, only the sacrifice of the Lamb of God, the Son of God, could take away sin. God looked on faith in his provision for their day—the animal substitute—as if it were faith in his Son. So in looking in faith to that substitute, old covenant believers were looking beyond it to the sacrifice of Christ.

All this sounds rather strange to our modern minds, but the very same principle applies today, though neither animal sacrifice nor a repeat or extension of Christ's once-for-all sacrifice is required. By his one all-sufficient sacrifice of himself, once offered, Christ has put an end to all other sacrifices for sin. But the benefits of his sacrifice are only applied to us when we come to him as sinners and confess our sins to him. 'If we say that we have no sin, we deceive ourselves, and the truth is not in us. If we confess our sins [directly to God], he is faithful and just to forgive us our sins, and to cleanse us from all unrighteousness' (1 John 1:8 AV).

God is faithful to his promise and he is just; since Christ has already paid the price of sin, he will not require us to pay it ourselves.

23

He died that we might be forgiven,
    He died to make us good;
That we might go at last to heaven
    Saved by his precious blood.

There was no other good enough
    To pay the price of sin;
He only could unlock the gate
    Of heaven and let us in.
                Cecil Frances Alexander, 1823-95

What must we do?

What must we do to be saved? The Bible makes it clear that we must do a great U-turn which it calls *repentance*. This was the keynote of the ministry of John the Baptist. The Bible presents him as the last in the line of those prophets sent by God to foretell Jesus Christ's coming. John was sent by God to clear the way for his Son. It is noticeable that repentance was the opening note of the Saviour's own ministry (Matthew 3:2-3; 4:17). It means turning away from our own way, from our selfishness and sins, and turning to the one who suffered for us and our sins. It means accepting what another has done for us (think about how that goes against the grain for the average person), and accepting free forgiveness for our sin. It means our lives are changed; we commit ourselves to going his way from now on. Only then can we find the peace the world cannot give and the peace the world cannot take away.

If you are not sure yet whether you have found this peace, let me urge you to make that U-turn. Repent of your sin and trust in Jesus' sacrifice for your salvation. The most important thing in the world for us is our relationship with

God. All too few seem to understand this. Why not find some quiet spot and turn to the Bible? Read again the story of that first Good Friday and ask yourself, Was this really for me? If so, isn't it time I did something about it? Each of the Gospel writers gives a vivid account of how it actually happened: Matthew in his chapters 26 and 27; Mark, as Peter saw it, in his chapters 14 and 15; Luke's careful examination of eye-witnesses in his chapters 22 and 23, and John, who crowns it all in his chapters 18 and 19 (don't stop there—you must go on to chapter 20).

Ask the living God to make the death of his Son real to you. Was there ever such love? 'For God so loved the world that he gave his only begotten [NIV one and only] Son, that whosoever believeth in him should not perish, but have everlasting life. For God sent not his Son into the world to condemn the world; but that the world through him might be saved' (John 3:16-17 AV).

Today would be a truly wonderful day for you if it turned out to be the day when you repented of your sin and called on the name of the Lord Jesus to save you! Two things would follow. You would want to tell someone you know (or suspect) has been praying for you. That would be a tremendous encouragement to them and would spur them on to continue to pray for others. The other thing is that you would want to tell someone you care for of your fresh discovery of God's way of salvation. Romans 10:8-13 gives us such encouragement to tell others of the great work that Christ has done for us. It is too important and too precious a matter to keep to ourselves. Such good news is for sharing with others, not keeping to ourselves.

3
What is the church?

The way we often use the word 'church' makes us believe that we can only worship God within a special building. We are all guilty of making this mistake. Local street maps mark the locations of such meeting places, all piles of bricks and mortar, steel and concrete. Although they may be different in their denomination, age, size, grandeur and available facilities, they are all central meeting places for worship. But in Acts 15:30 we are told, 'they gathered the church together'. You cannot do that with a building, only with people.

The English word 'church', like the Scottish word 'kirk' and the German word *Kirche*, comes from the Greek *kuriakos*, which means 'belonging to the *kurios*, the Lord'. The Greek word *ekklésia*, translated 'church', means an official assembly of people (literally 'called out'). In his first English translation William Tyndale consistently translated this word as 'congregation'. To have left it at that would have saved a lot of confusion. At the end of their gathering for public worship the church [congregation] would have been seen going down the street to its various homes. However, unless a distinction is made between what a building is used for and the people who assemble together in it, the confusion will probably remain.

Meeting God in a special place
There was a time when the people of God had to meet in a

26

special place. God gave them specific instructions to do so. After centuries of being slaves to the Egyptians, through the covenant God made with Moses the Israelites became a theocracy, a nation under the direct authority of God. They camped at Mount Sinai, and here God gave them instructions for the construction of a Tabernacle or a Tent, a special place central to their worship of God. It was built in such a way that it could be taken with them when they began their travels in the wilderness. The instructions were very detailed. Nothing was to be left to the people's imagination. They did as they were told (Exodus 25–29).

The Tabernacle appears to have been divided into two rooms by a curtain. In the outer room, or the Holy Place, certain articles of great significance were housed. In the inner room, the Most Holy Place or Holy of Holies, was the Ark of the Covenant or Testimony. The Ark in turn held certain special articles, all having great symbolism and meaning to the Israelites and central in their worship of God. Above the Ark shone the 'Glory of God' symbolised by two cherubim. We are told in Exodus 25:21-22, 'Place the cover on top of the ark and put in the ark the Testimony, which I will give you. There, above the cover between the two cherubim that are over the ark of the Testimony, I will meet with you and give you all my commands for the Israelites.'

The main function of the high priest was to mediate between God and man. It was to the Ark that the high priest went once a year on the Day of Atonement to sprinkle blood, both for himself and for the people. This had to be done year after year. Without this sacrifice the Israelites would have felt the full wrath of God and his consuming fire. No wonder, then, that the Tabernacle was such a special place. We too need a mediator. Today, no less than with the ancient Israelites, there is a gulf between God and people. This gulf is due to our sinfulness and God's holiness. The Bible tells us, 'your iniquities have separated you from your God' (Isaiah 59:2). Therefore we too need a High Priest, one who will bridge the gap and reconcile us to God. We need one who will remove the cause of the separation by doing all that is necessary to appease the holy God, offended by our disobedience and rebellion. Jesus Christ is that High Priest for his people; more, he himself was the sacrifice for our sins also. He did not bring the blood of a lamb to sprinkle before God, but his own blood as the Lamb of God. We are told in Hebrews 8:1-2 that our Great High Priest, Jesus Christ, has completed all that he came to do. 'We do have such a high priest, who sat down at the right hand of the throne of the Majesty in heaven, and who serves in the sanctuary, the true tabernacle set up by the Lord, not by man.'

Another meeting place for God's people was the Temple in Jerusalem. Unlike the Tabernacle it was not movable, but like the Tabernacle detailed instructions were given by God for its construction. Begun under king David and completed by his son Solomon, it was to be erected in a specific way, using materials chosen by God. It was far larger and grander than the Tabernacle constructed under the leadership of Moses, and it was to be the permanent home of the Ark of the Covenant. The people acknowledged that God's worthship (the origin of the word 'worship') was to be in a building set apart especially for this purpose.

During our Lord's ministry on earth there were synagogues (or places of gathering) dotted all over the land of Israel and throughout the Roman world. Christ had no problems using these buildings to speak of his Father. In Mark 1:39 we are told, 'So he travelled throughout Galilee, preaching in their synagogues and driving out demons.' But the Gospel records also tell us that the Lord preached often in the open air as well as in the synagogues. Think of the feeding of the five thousand recorded in Mark 6:30-44 and the feeding of the four thousand in Mark 8:1-10. Stephen tells us perfectly correctly that God does not now live in temples made by human hands. The death of Christ has done away with the need to have our sins dealt with in a special place within a Tabernacle or a Temple. In Mark 15:38 we are told that at the crucifixion of the Lord Jesus Christ the curtain of the Temple was torn in two, from top to bottom. We now have access to God through Christ and not through a special place of worship. He is our 'meeting place' with God (John 2:19-22).

Are we right then in saying that special buildings are unnecessary? Yes, they are unnecessary if we think of them as 'holy places', special places where we meet with God in a special way. Through Christ we can meet with God any-where and at any time. We can say, however, that central buildings are helpful, not because God is any more there than in any other building, but for purely practical reasons. There are buildings where believers come to worship God and where unbelievers can hear the gospel. But they are not an essential part of worship. Some churches decide not to own their building and instead hire schools, community halls, etc. This may be because they feel that the building has become too important in their thinking, or because it is causing too much of a financial drain on their resources. There are sound reasons for owning a building, and sound reasons for not doing so. But wherever we meet we must always remember that whatever the building, whatever its main purpose, only people who believe in Jesus can be called the true church of God in the New Testament use of the word. This is clearly seen in Matthew 18:20 where we are told, 'For where two or three come together in my name, there am I with them.'

Isaac Watts has it exactly right:

> Jesus, where'er Thy people meet,
> There they behold Thy mercy-seat;
> Where'er they seek Thee Thou art found,
> And every place is hallowed ground.
>
> For Thou, within no walls confined,
> Inhabitest the humble mind;
> Such ever bring Thee where they come,
> And going, take Thee to their home.

What is the church for?

Now that we have established what the church is, we must go on to ask what the church is for. Archbishop William Temple (1881-1944) said, 'The church is the only society in the world that exists for the benefit of non-members.' There is some truth in this statement, but not enough for the Christian to latch on to it as if it were the whole truth. In its well-meant endeavour to thrust evangelism to the fore, this comment fails to touch many Bible truths. It is true that many churches have no zeal for evangelism and are content to remain holy huddles, but it is equally true that the church does not exist for evangelism alone.

What function, then, ought the 'church' or a congregation of the Lord's people to exercise? What characteristics should it exhibit? It should be:

• *Noted for its prayer life* (Luke 19:46). Prayer, whether individual or corporate, is the pivot of the Christian life.

30

When we want to know how to pray we can do no better than take Jesus as our great example. He prayed on all occasions, often rising early in the morning when he knew he could spend time alone with his Father without the interruptions of others. He prepared himself for prayer before his Father so that he could both pray for himself and on behalf of others.

Some may wonder why our times of prayer at prayer meetings are so feeble. Could it be that vital preparation has been neglected? Perhaps we leave home in a rush or have our minds on other things. Or it may just be that our prayer life is almost totally non-existent, apart from the times when we come together with others for corporate prayer. We must always be determined to take part totally in public prayer, whether it be at the Sunday services or at the prayer meetings. Public prayer should be an extension of our private prayer. Time should be given over to the praise of our God, to prayer for revival, for world events, etc.—the list is endless. It is not the place for personal prayers. They are better said in private places. But both in private and public prayers access to God is the same; it is through our Lord and Saviour Jesus Christ who is the only mediator between God and man. We are now sons and daughters of God and have total access to him. We must remember in our public prayers to do nothing that makes it harder for others to concentrate on prayer. We do not come together to do our own thing, doing only what is right in our own eyes. What each of us does as an individual affects others and may cause great distraction.

The early churches were known for their coming together in prayer. In Acts 1 amazing things happened to them. The apostles had seen the Lord taken up to heaven before their eyes. Angels had spoken to them. We might expect that such great events would be discussed and analysed. It would appear not. The first recorded thing the disciples did after returning to Jerusalem was to meet together for prayer. In Acts 1:14 we are told, 'They all joined together constantly in prayer, along with the women and Mary the mother of Jesus, and with his brothers.' That could certainly teach us all a lesson.

• *Committed to public preaching.* It is the role of those in leadership in a local church to ensure that the preaching of the gospel is an integral and regular part of the church's worship and practice. Because Christ has been given authority by his Father, we, in turn, can proclaim the gospel to others with total assurance. We are not simply passing on a fable or a fairy story but the Word of Truth. We are told in Matthew 28:18-19,

> Then Jesus came to them and said, 'All authority in heaven and on earth has been given to me. Therefore go and make disciples of all nations, baptising them in the name of the Father and of the Son and of the Holy Spirit, and teaching them to obey everything I have commanded you. And surely I am with you always, to the very end of the age.'

We must do as we are commanded.

• *Characterised by discipline within scriptural principles.* In 1 Corinthians 5:1-5 we are told about a type of sexual immorality that had developed within the church, such that not even the outside world would accept. The church was severely criticised by Paul for not only ignoring this sinful act but also for seemingly being proud of it. It is never easy to take a brother or sister in the Lord to task, but it is something that is necessary as a part of church discipline in order to bring the problem out into the open and achieve a resolution of the issue. Only when this happens can the person concerned come in true repentance to the living God. It is no use hiding a problem under the carpet—it is not the way for it to be dealt with. Yet, on the other hand, the church is not to be harshly authoritarian in its exercise of discipline (see 2 Corinthians 2:5-7; Romans 15:1-7).

• *Marked by fellowship in a memorial feast.* Our Communion Table with its bread and wine carries memorials to the death of our Lord. These are offered to believers to eat and drink, not to save them from sin but to remind them of Christ's amazing love in giving himself as their Redeemer. In 1 Corinthians 11:20-34 we are told of the way the memorial supper is to be taken. Verses 20-22 tell us it is not a meal to satisfy our bodies. Verses 23-26 tell us the bread and wine are symbols of the broken body and shed blood of the Lord Jesus Christ for the sins of his people. Verses 27-28 warn us not to eat it in an unworthy manner but to examine ourselves before we partake. We are told especially in verse 29 that one who takes the bread and wine but does not accept that Christ died for his sins 'eats and drinks judgment on himself'—a reminder that a warning should be given every time the Lord's Supper takes place. Bishop Latimer (1485–1555) taught the priests in Worcester to say at the communion service

> Of Christ's body this is a token,
> Which on the cross for sins was broken;
> Wherefore of your sins you must be forsakers
> If of His life you would be partakers.

• *Recognised as a people who are joyful.* Without a real knowledge of the Lord Jesus Christ it is impossible to know the joy of the Lord—not the joy of the world that bursts its bubble when the tough times come, but the inner peace that comes from a right relationship with our Lord. We cannot always be smiling and laughing. This is not real joy anyway. Activities and incidents crowd in upon us that often make us very sad. But over and over again we are told of the great joy that the writers of the Scriptures had, especially when they were working for and worshipping their Lord. Often this joy exhibited itself in remarkable circumstances. Paul could speak about praying 'with joy' (Philippians 1:4). It did not matter even if he was in prison, he could still bear the same joyous testimony (see Acts 16:25). Fellowship with the Lord and his people is something that should always be exhibited when we come together for worship. We do not have to jump up and down or clap our hands to be joyful; it will be shown in our singing and on our faces.

• *Identified as a people who love one another.* In 1 John 2:9-11 we are told that this special love is a mark of a true Christian. Those who do not show it cannot claim this name:

Anyone who claims to be in the light but hates his brother is still in the darkness. Whoever loves his brother lives in the light, and there is nothing in him to make him stumble (vv.9-10).

Christian love embraces not just our like-minded fellow believers but all our brothers and sisters in Christ, however different some of them may be from us. All for whom our Saviour died are to be the objects of our love, for we belong to the same family. This love will manifest itself in many ways, both spiritual and practical, but it must be in evidence if we call ourselves Christians.

• *Acknowledged as a people who are taught and trained.* The New Testament is full of examples of the teaching of both Christ and his disciples. We can never have enough of sound biblical teaching. Never assume that you have arrived at a point where you cannot learn anything new. The so-called wise of our day may mock us for believing in the God of creation and insisting that the Lord Jesus is absolutely unique, the only Saviour of the world. But the teaching we receive from the Bible is final and utterly true. The form our corporate worship service takes will vary from church to church. This does not matter so much as long as it is known that when we come together we will receive teaching that is faithfully based on the Word of God. When the teaching is squeezed into a ten-minute talk that is more suitable for children, then we are heading for great problems. Sound doctrinal teaching is one way these can be avoided. Ephesians 4:14 says,

> Then we will no longer be infants, tossed back and forth by the waves, and blown here and there by every wind of teaching and by the cunning and craftiness of men in their deceitful scheming. Instead, speaking the truth in love, we will in all things grow up into him who is the Head, that is, Christ.

A church that is not soundly taught is one that will be open to the wiles of the devil as he stalks to find his prey. There is a war on. Satan and all his demonic forces are seeking to frustrate the worldwide purposes of our great God and

Saviour. We must never forget that 'our struggle is not against flesh and blood, but against the rulers, against the authorities, against the powers of this dark world and against the spiritual forces of evil in the heavenly realms' (Ephesians 6:12). We need to be taught and trained to face the invisible foe and stand as victors in the final day.

• *Burning with zeal to make Christ known.* He commanded us to make disciples of all nations (Matthew 28:19). Yet as we near the end of the second millennium there are still people groups who have never heard the gospel. And there are many in our own community who have never been witnessed to by a Christian believer. We need to pray for the evangelistic zeal of those early Christians who, scattered by persecution from Jerusalem, 'preached the word wherever they went' (Acts 8:4).

4
Is the devil real?

Whatever people today may say about the devil, he is neither a myth nor a figment of an over-zealous imagination. Nor is he to be joked over, toyed with or made fun of. The devil is very real. He is a totally evil being with a variety of deadly aims. His very essence is evil and his nature comprises pride and conceit. We know this to be true because the Bible says that those being considered for the office of elder should not be recent converts or they 'may become conceited and fall under the same judgment as the devil' (1 Timothy 3:6).

The devil's aims
What are the devil's aims?

His first purpose is to make God out to be a liar. This is brought out clearly in Genesis 3:1. He accosts the woman Eve, the high creation of God's hand, and challenges the Creator's authority. 'Did God really say, "You must not eat from any tree in the garden"?' He implies, then categorically declares, that God cannot be trusted.

His next aim is to deceive unbelievers into thinking that they can manage their life and death quite happily without God's intervention. They may hear the Word of God preached or have a Christian friend speak about it to them, but 'Satan comes and takes away the word that was sown in them' (Mark 4:15). In its place the devil puts the thought that God and his message are unnecessary.

The devil also aims to make the lives of believers as unproductive as possible. All men begin under the mastery and bondage of Satan. Only God can bring release and freedom. When he does, Christians—for that is what they become—are free to follow after God and worship him. The devil hates to lose his prey and therefore endeavours to cause divisions and schisms between Christians. He puts obstacles in the way of believers carrying out their Christian tasks. For example, in 1 Thessalonians 2:18 Paul writes, 'Satan stopped us', and in 2 Corinthians 12:7 Paul experiences 'a thorn in my flesh, a messenger of Satan, to torment me'. Yet, however painful these limitations may be, God does not let Satan have full rein. The Lord permitted Satan to afflict Job and bring him right down to rock-bottom, but he would not allow Satan to take his life from him. The Lord alone has the power over life and death.

The strongest reason for believing that the devil is real is that Christ himself experienced attacks by the devil. Frontal attacks occurred in the forty days the Lord was in the wilderness. Mark and Luke both record this experience, but its source must have been the Lord himself, because he was alone in the wilderness when the temptations occurred. Our Lord suffered another attack by the devil through Peter. When Jesus tells his disciples about his future suffering and death in Matthew 16:21, Peter is adamant that this will not happen. Jesus sees the devil at work and says, 'Get behind me, Satan!' It seems that this was not just Peter being misguided in his ideas, but the devil actually working through him, trying to obstruct Christ's progress to the cross and to make his work on earth come to nothing.

The great imitator
We must remember that everything God does the devil

parodies. The devil is a great imitator. God has Christ: the devil has his antichrists. We are told in 1 John 4:3 that 'every spirit that does not acknowledge Jesus is not from God. This is the spirit of the antichrist.' Or in 2 John verse 7: 'Many deceivers, who do not acknowledge Jesus Christ as coming in the flesh, have gone out into the world. Any such person is the deceiver and the antichrist.' Christ alone achieved all he set out to do. Antichrists cannot achieve any more than God will allow.

Christ was God incarnate: the devil has his 'incarnations' through demon-possession, or possession by evil spirits. An example of demon-possession is found in Matthew 15:22 when the Canaanite woman cried out for Jesus to heal her daughter.

The Saviour suffered a vicarious death, and he instituted the Communion Table or the Lord's Supper. Satanists copy both of these in their ritual sacrifices and black masses.

The Lord Jesus and his disciples performed many miracles while they were on earth. The pages of the Gospels are full of signs and wonders, too many to number. But why were they performed and recorded? We are told in John 20:31 it was so that we may 'believe that Jesus is the Christ, the Son of God, and that by believing [we] may have life in his name'. In John 3:3 Nicodemus, a Pharisee, testifies that 'no-one could perform the miraculous signs you are doing if God were not with him'. Yet we must also remember that the devil also performs great signs and wonders. Christ warns of deceivers that will appear 'in the last days'. As recorded in Matthew 24:24 Christ says, 'For false Christs and false prophets will appear and perform great signs and miracles to deceive even the elect—if that were possible.' The Saviour has warned us ahead of time—we cannot say we have not been warned.

God has his good angels, sent forth to minister to all those who will inherit salvation (Hebrews 1:14). It appears that the devil has his evil angels. The Greek word for angel is literally translated as 'messenger'. Sometimes these evil angels appear as angels of light. Those who do not preach the gospel of Christ in its entirety and totality may well be such 'angels of light', or messengers of the devil. In 2 Corinthians 11:4, 13-15, Paul warns his readers,

> For if someone comes to you and preaches a Jesus other than the Jesus we preached [the Jesus of the Bible] . . . such men are false apostles, deceitful workmen, masquerading as apostles of Christ. And no wonder, for Satan himself masquerades as an angel of light. It is not surprising, then, if his servants masquerade as servants of righteousness.

God has sent forth his Holy Spirit. The devil sends out lying spirits. He plans evil acts, immorality, degradation and depravity. The greater the activity of Satan, the more a government changes its laws in ways that differ from the laws of God. The moral fabric of a society is weakened, good becomes evil and evil good, and the very distinction between right and wrong becomes unclear.

The devil's devices
The devil is always seeking to divide societies, churches and familes. When he fails to divide, he seeks to divert, so that unbelievers begin to doubt his existence and Christians start to concentrate on non-essentials.

The devil also tries his utmost to smear God's character. He makes out either that God is a hard taskmaster, a tyrant bent on making our lives miserable, or else that he is too soft-hearted to condemn anybody for anything. He specialises in casting doubts on God's power, wisdom, justice and love. He asks how a good, loving God could allow people to be killed accidentally or to die of cancer at a young age.

The devil plays on our natural characteristics. If we tend to be sceptical, he will tempt us to doubt the supernatural. He allows us to accept that psychologists have found a natural, rational explanation for everything. If we are scientifically minded he tempts us to dismiss the story of creation as nothing more than a Hebrew myth, or else go to the other extreme and take the Bible as nothing more than a very early scientific textbook. If we tend to be legalistic, then the devil will try and persuade us that being sound in doctrine is everything and that behaviour is unimportant. If we are gentle by nature, then the devil will encourage our non-judgmental characteristic and put it in our minds that 'love is everything, and truth divides'.

The devil is always trying to make us procrastinate, persuading us there is plenty of time left in which souls can be saved. Did you hear the story about the council meeting in hell? The demons had all been summoned by the devil. He took the chair. The object of the exercise was to find the best way of defeating the church. One demon said, 'Let's deny the Virgin Birth'. 'And the atoning death of Christ', said another. 'And his bodily resurrection', added a third. 'Let's say there is nothing after death, and certainly no day of judgment', added yet another. So they went on, suggesting one vital doctrine after another. But finally, one demon suggested that they should agree that all these things were true, but that folk should not take them too seriously, because there was still plenty of time. At that there was a standing ovation. They all felt this demon had hit the jackpot. The story may sound far-fetched, but there is no denying that if doubt slays its thousands, procrastination slays its tens of thousands. It is one of Satan's best and most deadly weapons.

At work today

The devil is very much at work in the world today. Many of the dreadful things that are happening are a result of the powers of darkness at work in the world. It is not just a matter of awkward personalities, political clashes, ambition and ethnic or personal pride, economic difficulties and industrial problems. It is the heavy hand of the devil himself, seeking to wreck the whole of mankind and foil the Creator's plans for peace (1 Timothy 2:1-8). Think of the various wars that have taken place in our world over the past fifty years. Who in the whole wide world really wants the havoc and devastation, the misery and bitterness that war inevitably brings? Are we not appalled by the regular pictures of long straggling lines of civilians fleeing for refuge and looking for food? Behind all this are Satanic forces interested in nothing less than the destruction of mankind and the thwarting of the purpose of the living God for the good of his creation.

Our Lord teaches clearly that the kingdom of God is opposed by an enemy who is the head of a powerful force. Happily this head is not all-powerful; only Christ is omnipotent. The enemy is also not all-knowing; only Christ is omniscient. He is not everywhere at the same time; only Christ is omnipresent. The devil can only reach many people at the same time by using his emissaries, the demons. They seek to do the devil's work for him. It is Satan who encourages, through his minions (see *The Screwtape Letters* by C. S. Lewis), the spirit of fear, jealousy, lust, immorality, and all

42

the other spirits which crawl out of his kingdom. But thank God, the Lord Jesus is not only able to come to the rescue of Christians under satanic attack, he is able to set free captive men and women who are ensnared by evil spirits. He can evict Satan's powerful lodgers. He is able to subdue all things unto himself.

The devil and his angels have a very dreadful place reserved for them. In Matthew 25:41 we read, 'Depart from me, you who are cursed, into the eternal fire prepared for the devil and his angels.' The words 'eternal' and 'fire' should be enough to send shivers of dread on all those who hear them and understand their full implications. As we have said, the devil is no fool; he knows what will happen to him. Until that day he will take no rest as he goes about the land, causing as much destruction and devastation as he possibly can.

Because the evil powers we are up against are so strong, so subtle, so vastly experienced, we must be constantly on our guard. No wonder the apostle Paul urges us to come constantly to the Lord for strength that is greater than our own. Only in this way, confessing our utter dependence on him, can we stand against the wiles or strategies of the devil. Only in the strength of the risen and ascended Lord can we stand our ground and emerge as victors over all the powers of darkness (Ephesians 6:10-18).

Let us then serve the Lord while we can, and serve him with all our heart, soul, mind and strength. Let us be strong in the Lord and in the power of his might. Satan is powerful, stronger, more experienced, more subtle, than any human being. But he has not been given all power in heaven and on earth. That belongs to our Saviour alone: 'All authority in heaven and on earth has been given to me' (Matthew 28:18).

The devil is real; but greater far is the one who must reign until he puts all his enemies—the devil included—under his feet (1 Corinthians 15:25; compare Revelation 20:10).

5
What about hell?

It is commonly held that intelligent and informed people do not believe in a place called hell. Some say there is no God and therefore fearing hell or hoping for heaven are pointless. Hell to them is no more than a big joke, something to make fun of. It is seen as a fairy story or myth, a magic kingdom ruled over by the devil, a creature with horns and a tail who goes about causing as much havoc as possible. He is viewed in the same way as dragons and monsters, elves and hobgoblins.

Still others hold the view that the whole idea of hell is nothing more than a psychological lever, a sort of religious bluff on a par with a parent's empty threat trying to stop a naughty child from doing something wrong. Such a ploy is unworthy of the God of truth. Would God give us empty promises or warn us of non-existent dangers?

But varying views on hell are not limited to those who do not believe in God. We get some very different answers when we ask 'religious' people about hell. The answer will vary according to how seriously they take the Bible. Some will say that the only hell we have is here on earth. When life goes wrong and you make a mess of it, that's hell. Or if life 'treats you badly', that's hell. Others will say that everything about hell in the Gospels has been imported from Judaism. Matthew and Mark could not forget their Jewish prejudices, ideas they had picked up from their pre-Christian teachers. They have put into the Saviour's mouth hard sayings he would never have uttered.

All the cults, too, have their version of what hell is like. For example, Christian Scientists believe it is 'self-imposed agony'. Jehovah's Witnesses say we will all be given a 'second chance' to put ourselves right with God, and none but a few will be so stupid as to throw this second opportunity of heaven away. As hell is seen as nothing more than death and the grave anyway, the thought of it is not really too awful. However, when we go through the creeds of the various religions and cults of the world we discover that those who founded them did so on the whim of man and not on the basis of a holy God. They each have deficient and defective doctrines of sin which culminate in a wrong view of hell. It is because nobody likes the idea of separation and eternal damnation from God that the Bible's realism has been watered down.

Many evangelicals now teach that while there is such a place as hell, sinners only go there as a punishment for a limited period of time. If you have not been particularly wicked, you only go for a short while and are then annihilated. If you qualify for the longer treatment, your annihilation is delayed much longer. Hell, yes. Pain, yes. Endless pain, no!

• **What does the Bible say?**
The really important question is, What does the Bible say about hell?

The first thing we can say is that whatever the Bible says about hell is true. Christians who take the Bible as their authority in all matters of faith and conduct have no option but to accept that there is a biblical doctrine of hell. Those who do so may be a small minority in our land today, but their convictions have been held by faithful believers in every generation since the time of the apostles. I believe with all my heart that the Scriptures are absolutely true in all they say, but I still shrink from the implications of what I read as readily as anyone who is sensitive to the thought of people suffering. Nevertheless, to believe the Gospel records as being the true account of what Christ says about hell is the only position that can be taken by those who believe the Bible is the Word of God. What our Lord says on any subject has final authority, no matter how unpalatable it may seem to be or how unpopular it may be with our contemporaries. As surely as there is a heaven to be sought, there is a hell to be shunned. There is a place after death for those who have rejected Christ while they lived on earth. Christ is the Father's appointed 'door to heaven'.

We have to establish, however, that there are different words used in the Bible to describe where both believers and unbelievers go after death. At death all bodies, both of believers and unbelievers alike, remain where they have been laid to rest and revert to dust. The souls of believers go directly to be with the Lord. We read this in Luke 23:43 where the Lord tells the dying thief, 'I tell you the truth, today you will be with me in paradise'. Paradise is heaven but without our present bodies. We are not given a detailed description of what Paradise will be like, but we know, because we will be in the presence of our Lord, that when we get there it will be the only place that we will want to be. The different names given to hell are far more complicated. In his book *Whatever happened to hell?* John Blanchard gives a detailed description of what he calls 'the hell of words': Sheol, an Old Testament description, Hades and Gehenna. It may be that you wish to undertake further study on this subject. However, for the sake of simplicity, I am going to render each as 'hell'.

So I ask again—what does the Bible teach us about hell?

1. There is an unbridgeable chasm between heaven and hell. In Luke 16:19-31 we are told the story of the rich man and the beggar Lazarus. The rich man badly wanted to warn his family about hell, but Abraham told him that 'between us and you a great chasm has been fixed, so that those who want to go from here to you cannot, nor can anyone cross over from there to us' (verse 26).

At first glance it may seem hard that no warning is to be allowed. However, Abraham goes on to explain that they have warnings a plenty in 'Moses and the Prophets' (verse 29), but they have taken no notice of them, and even if 'someone rises from the dead they will not be convinced' (verse 31). The chasm is fixed. There is only one life in which to warn those of the eternal punishment to come.

This concept of a 'fixed chasm' rules out any possibility of the dead in hell being able to communicate with the living on earth. Spiritism suggest that all those who are dead are 'floating around' in some world beyond ours. This is not so. Spiritism is not the communication between the living and the dead but between the living and demons or evil spirits. These are in the employment of the devil and do much of his work of deception for him. Christians are never to indulge in this type of behaviour and we are to warn all others against doing so.

2. There is no freedom in hell. John Blanchard demonstrates that hell differs from an earthly prison, even though the two are sometimes compared. But prison can only confine the body, not the mind. Even in the smallest, dampest, darkest cell, devoid of adequate food and drink, with nothing to occupy either body or mind, the mind is still free to roam over the past, present and future as it wills. Hell demands all our body, mind and soul. There is no escape of the mind into other realms. John Blanchard comes to the conclusion that 'Hell will make the worst earthly prison seem like a holiday camp.'

3. Hell is a place of great and eternal darkness. We are told many times in Scripture that darkness is reserved for those who have no time for God or who go against his laws and precepts. We do not know if this darkness is physical, but we do know that it is somewhere where God's face will be hidden. Over and over again in Scripture we read that 'light' is a representation of all that is right and good, and 'darkness' of all that is evil and bad. 1 John 1:5 says, 'God is light; in him there is no darkness at all. If we claim to have fellowship with hm yet walk in darkness, we lie and do not live by the truth.' In John 1:5 we read, 'The light shines in the darkness, but the darkness has not understood it.' The light referred to here is Christ. In Matthew 5:14 believers are referred to as 'light'. 'You are the light of the world. A city on a hill cannot be hidden.' Hell, then, as a place of darkness would appear to be devoid of God, Christ, believers, and hope.

4. Hell is a place of fire. The worm does not die and the fire never goes out. Matthew 5:22; 18:8; 25:41 and Jude v.7 all warn us of the fire of hell. Fire is a terrifying element. On earth fire can both purify and destroy. But the fire of hell does neither. Imagine the unspeakable horror of being caught in a fire that did not destroy you but just kept on burning. In that circumstance death would come as a welcome release.

5. Hell is a place of agony of mind. We have already looked at this aspect before, but there is more we can say about it. All in hell will know why they are there and will want to warn others on earth of what is to come. But they will not be able to do so. Nor would it do any good if they could. Perhaps a striking analogy will convey this tragic fix. Imagine, all in very slow motion, seeing a child running into the path of a lorry. You try and scream but the child does not hear you. The two come together so very slowly that the time/space ratio cannot be measured. You know one day they will collide, but you can neither stop it or turn your eyes away from it. A real torment of mind.

• **Is hell 'for ever'?**
It is significant that the word translated as 'punishment' in Matthew 25:46 (*kolasis*) is used in modern Greek for 'hell'. And it is equally significant that the Greek word for 'everlasting' found in the AV of the same verse is the same word as that for 'eternal'. The one is as long-lasting as the other. In Mark 9:48 we are solemnly told that hell is a place 'where the worm does not die, and the fire is not quenched'. The sense of loss will go on for ever, never dying. Once you have entered into it, there is no escape to a better place. The response to those who are sure that their understanding of biblical teaching allows for a limited period in hell must be that we take Scripture as it is, not as we want it to be. Heaven is a perfect place. Perfect fellowship, perfect worship, perfect service and perfect peace. No one would ever want to leave, for it is here that the believer will worship and have communion for ever with his God and with fellow saints. Hell is also for ever, but it is very different. Forget the bad jokes about hell being a place full of like-minded people enjoying an eternity of riotous 'living'. Hell

50

will be so unimaginably dreadful that nothing will be further from their minds.

• **Who is hell for?**

Man was intended for spiritual union with God, both on earth and in heaven. However, we read in Genesis 3 how sin entered into the world. Man was deceived by the devil. Every man, woman and child who has been born ever since has been born a sinner into a sinful world. There is no escape from this. But God, being totally and absolutely just and righteous, can have nothing to do with sin. To do so would be outside of his nature. It is only the God of biblical Christianity who is so perfect and just that he cannot tolerate sin. It is this God who is righteously angry because of sin, and whose justice demands that he ought to send all who have sinned to hell—that means all who have ever lived. We read in Romans 3:23, 'for all have sinned and fall short of the glory of God'.

But this same God of biblical Christianity has made a way back to him possible; his justice and judgment, wrath and condemnation are mixed with mercy and grace and patience. Through the death on the cross of his Son, the Lord Jesus Chrst, God has secured a way of reconciliation, a way of salvation. The Bible explains clearly and simply. We cannot claim that it is not fair or that we did not know. (See Ezekiel chapters 18 and 33.)

God has warned us that if we sin and do not repent of it, then we will go to hell. The language is clear. It is not just the dreadful, heinous crimes that send us to hell, for every transgression of God's holy law and moral standard opens us individually to the wrath of God. But more than this, our very nature, opposed to God and rebellious against his directions and intructions, is inherently biased to evil. In

51

the first instance we sin because we are sinners. While we will be judged individually for what we have done we will go to hell for what we are—sinners in the sight of a holy God.

Let the artists and the novelists conjure up their ideas of what hell will be like; nothing on earth can fully capture the horror that it is and everlastingly will be. Someone has said, 'We would have to be there to know fully how dreadful it is.'

6
What about those who have never heard the gospel?

'Do you mean to tell me that God will condemn to hell for ever a sincere Muslim who, through absolutely no fault of his own, has never heard the gospel? Because, if so, I don't want your God!' So said an angry student to a missionary.

Popular opinion is very much on the side of the student. Many religious teachers who would claim the title 'Christian' leave the impression that a man will not be condemned unless he has heard and understood the Christian gospel. The logical consequence of this is the attitude, 'Leave the heathen alone. They're better off as they are. Why increase their responsibility and the possibility of their condemnation?'

So the sense of urgency to make Christ known in all the world evaporates. Young people, especially the men, settle down to easy-going, remunerative jobs at home. The search for comfort and security precludes their going very far in search of 'the lost'. 'Why go abroad? There are enough heathen here. I'm needed here', is the usual excuse.

The modern world is also intolerant of intolerance. People reason like this:

—You can believe you're right if you like, but *you mustn't say that all the others are wrong*. A comparative study of religions leaves no room for bigotry or the claim that any one religion is unique. Man is a religious animal. His creative urges constantly give him fresh insights into the nature of God. Christianity is one insight and it suits the Western mind very well. Hinduism and Buddhism are other insights and they suit the Eastern world better.

—*As long as a man lives up to the light he has,* he'll be all right. One man's meat is another man's poison. After all, it's mainly a matter of upbringing. You believe what you're brought up to believe. Why go around interfering with other people's beliefs?

—*Truth has myriad fragments.* Try to fit in the bits you have with the bits other men have. Synthesis is not only desirable but attainable with patience. We'll come to it sooner or later, if not in our day. The world religion is coming up over the horizon.

—You don't mean to say you believe that *millions of people are lost* just because they're not Christians? What an appalling suggestion! Why, many of them haven't even heard of Christianity! How dare you suggest that Christianity is the only way to God?

How should Christians answer such arguments as these? Firstly, we should seek to ask and answer several fundamental questions. Who are the heathen? What do the masses of people know about God before they hear the Christian message? What does the Bible teach about the heathen? What is the Christian's duty towards those who have never heard of Christ?

• **Who are the heathen?**
If we think at all about the heathen, we may very probably think of them as those who worship idols. And until quite

recently Christians in the West tended to think of them as a long way from us geographically.

Here, however, I am using the word heathen to refer to the multitudes who have no knowledge of the Lord Jesus Christ. This, of course, includes the heathen in the Western world who may have some knowledge of Christianity but have no time for it. My definition, therefore, is broader than the *Oxford Dictionary*'s, 'Neither Christian, Jewish, nor Muslim'. It allows that there may be many practical heathens in the 'Christian' United Kingdom, as in countries dominated by non-Christian religions.

• **What do the heathen know about God?**
Many missionaries point out that the so-called heathen know more than we think. They know that there is a God. 'There are no atheists among heathen tribes,' writes C. C. Weiss. 'There has never been discovered upon the face of the earth a tribe of people, however small or depraved, which has not believed in some kind of god or had some system of worship.'

Where has this knowledge come from? The answer is that God has written on the human heart a consciousness of himself and his law. When the Bible speaks of the heart it generally includes the conscience. The heathen are not clear about God's personality and nature, but they are confident that 'there is something somewhere'. The polytheist's one-god-per-phenomenon (rain, rivers, trees, etc.) is the logical outcome of the conviction that there is a god in everything. The animist's worship of sun, stars and sticks shows ignorance of God's nature but awareness of his existence in many forms.

The heathen found in so-called primitive tribes know that they have sinned. When a Christian missionary comes to them and talks about sin, he often finds them ready to admit that they are sinners. They often seem to know that their sin must be punished. They seem afraid of punishment, and afraid of death, as are most men everywhere if they are honest with themselves. They know that sin must be atoned for, and they seek ways of appeasing their angry deities or deity. But they don't know of Christ, his atonement for sin, his victory over death, and their need to come to him for salvation.

• **Some key issues**

The Scriptures give no support whatever for the idea that heathen worship is a stage in the upward surging of humanity. The Bible depicts no embryonic condition of man with hope for development. Rather,

> men . . . by their wickedness suppress the truth. For what can be known about God is plain to them, because God has shown it to them. Ever since the creation of the world his invisible nature, namely, his eternal power and deity, has been clearly perceived in the things that have been made. So they are without excuse; for although they knew God they did not honour him as God or give thanks to him, but they became futile in their thinking and their senseless minds were darkened. Claiming to be wise, they became fools, and exchanged the glory of the immortal God for images resembling mortal man or birds or animals or reptiles. Therefore God gave them up in the lusts of their hearts to impurity, to the dishonouring of their bodies among themselves, because they exchanged the truth about God for a lie and worshipped and served the creature rather than the Creator . . . For this reason God gave them up to dishonourable passions . . . (Romans 1:18-26 RSV).

56

According to Scripture—the final authority for the Christian faith—the heathen do not know God personally but use vain repetitions that are never heard. Like all non-Christians, the heathen are 'dead in trespasses [going across boundaries God has placed] and sins [falling short of the standards God has set]' and are 'by nature, children of wrath', i.e. worthy of God's righteous displeasure. They are 'perishing', 'blinded', and under the dominion of darkness (Jeremiah 10:25; Matthew 6:7; Ephesians 2:1-5; 2 Corinthians 2:15; 4:4; Colossians 1:13).

Sick and without strength, powerless to save themselves, they cannot possibly live up to the light they have. Being by nature enemies of the living God, they 'live in the futility of their minds; they are darkened in their understanding, alienated from the life of God because of the ignorance that is in them, due to the hardness of their heart' (Ephesians 4:17,18). They give themselves to urges that call upon the basest part of their nature and give rein to their lust, in thought if not in word and deed. Wherever there is idolatry, there will be immorality (Ephesians 5:6-10).

Perhaps you feel the above descriptions are exaggerated, and you may answer, 'They are not all like this.' But the Scripture says, 'There is no distinction, since all have sinned and fall short of the glory of God . . . ' (Romans 3:22,23 RSV), and

None is righteous, no, not one; no one understands, no one seeks for God. All have turned aside, together they have gone wrong; no one does good, not even one . . . in their paths are ruin and misery, and the way of peace they do not know (Romans 3:10-17 RSV).

The problem is not really, Why should the heathen be lost? so much as, How could a holy God justify anyone?

57

What is strange is not that some should be lost, but that any should be saved.

Some Christians divide the heathen into two groups:

- those who deliberately reject Christ when his offers and claims are intelligently presented, who therefore deserve no further chance beyond this life; and

- those who cannot be blamed for not accepting what they have not heard, who, some folk feel, are bound to get a second chance after death.

But there are certain important questions we must face before we could accept such a conclusion.

1. *Does Scripture contain any hint that there will be a further opportunity for repentance and faith for anyone after death?* Christ's story of Lazarus and the rich man (Luke 16:19-31) indicates the exact opposite. Certain verses written by the apostle Peter—1 Peter 3:18-20 and 4:6—are often brought up by advocates of a second chance. But regardless of whether the preaching was through Christ's Spirit speaking in Noah, or later, between his death and resurrection, the context gives no hint of a 'second chance' or of conversion after death. Further, the second chance idea contradicts the clear biblical statement: 'It is appointed unto men once to die, but after this the judgment' (Hebrews 9:27). If the Lord and his disciples believed in a second chance after death, why did they not say something about it instead of giving such solemn teaching as this?

If your hand causes you to sin, cut it off; it is better for you to enter life maimed than with two hands to go to hell, to the unquenchable fire. And if your foot causes you to sin, cut it off; it is better for you to enter life lame than with two feet to be thrown into hell. And if your eye causes you to sin, pluck it out; it is better for you to enter into the kingdom of God with one eye than with two eyes to be thrown into hell, where their worm does not die, and the fire is not quenched (Mark 9:43-48). (See also Acts 13:40,41; 17:30,31.)

2. *If a man lived up to his light, how would he stand with God?* The crucial passage here seems to be Romans 2:12-16. (See also 2:25; 10:5.) Does this mean that those who live up to the law will be accounted righteous under the law? Scripture says little about this, almost certainly because of the answer to the next question.

3. *Does anyone actually live up to his light, not just in moral excellence but in relation to God?* In Romans 3 and Galatians 3 the apostle Paul gives us the Christian answer. Of all those born on earth, only Christ has never sinned. No one else has an absolutely clear conscience before God. Christ reminded his hearers that the first and great commandment is to love God with all your heart and mind and soul and strength (Mark 12:29,30). Who of us can plead that we are 'not guilty' of breaking this commandment? Our secret life cannot stand up to his all-seeing eyes. 'We have all become like one who is unclean, and all our righteous deeds are like a polluted garment. We all fade like a leaf, and our iniquities, like the wind, take us away' (Isaiah 64:6).

4. *If all of us need forgiveness, what is the ground of forgiveness?* How may we find it? Forgiveness is not given to people for doing their best to keep the law they have. Forgiveness is to be found only through Christ's merits. If it could have been found in any other way, would God have sent his Son to that awful, lonely death? He died that we

might be forgiven. The condemnation due to us fell upon him. There is no other way. 'And there is salvation in no one else, for there is no other name under heaven given among men by which we must be saved' (Acts 4:12). He is the only mediator with God. 'There is one God, and there is one mediator between God and men, the man Christ Jesus, who gave himself as a ransom for all' (1 Tim. 2:5,6). He is the only way to God. We find forgiveness when we turn from our sins and our self-centred way of living and trust him as our Saviour and Lord (John 14:6; 10:9,10; Romans 3:21-26).

5. *Could not sincerity or faithfulness to another religion be a substitute for faith in Christ?* What about the sincere Muslim? Many scriptures give an unequivocal answer to these questions. 'He who believes in the son has eternal life; he who does not obey the Son shall not see life, but the wrath of God rests upon him' (John 3:36, and note also other verses referred to in the preceding paragraph). There is no hint that even a sincere Jew could be saved by his sincerity or ethical standards or religious observances. Peter, a Jew, speaking to Jews, says, 'But we believe that we shall be saved through the grace of the Lord Jesus, just as they [the Gentiles] will' (Acts 15:11; cf. Galatians 3:21-24).

6. *Can those ignorant of the gospel be saved apart from explicit faith in Christ?* The operative word here is 'explicit'. Paul says that those who obstruct the preaching of the gospel not only displease God but act against the best interests of all men, 'hindering us from speaking to the Gentiles that they may be saved' (1 Thessalonians 2:16). Hearing the gospel is essential.

. . . 'every one who calls upon the name of the Lord will be saved.' But how are men to call upon him in whom they have not believed? And how are they to believe in him of whom they have never heard? And how are they to hear without a preacher? And how can men preach unless they are sent? (Rom. 10:13-15 RSV).

Also, the great commission presupposes that there is no safety in ignorance (Matthew 28:19,20; cf. 2 Corinthians 4:3,4; Romans 1:18-20), and in Acts 20:26,27 Paul takes up Ezekiel 3:7-21 which gives us our position today: Christians are placed by God as watchmen to bear witness to all men.

Some hold that 'ignorant heathen' are in a position analogous to that of the Old Testament patriarchs (for example, Abraham as related in Romans 4, especially verse 3), so that if they throw themselves in repentance upon the mercy of God, they will find forgiveness and be saved eternally through the death of Christ in spite of their ignorance in this world. There was a sense in which Cornelius was 'accepted' by God before he heard the gospel (Acts 10:34,35). But church history has few Corneliuses. And Cornelius needed the gospel before he could receive power to live for Christ through the Spirit. God sometimes speaks to people through dreams, as we read in Job 33:14-30, and some missionaries have found the way paved for their ministry by a vivid dream someone remembered. But the gospel was still needed to bring peace to the troubled conscience and power to the feeble will. Romans 10:9-14 seems to teach clearly that people must hear the gospel to be saved. Those dying in infancy and those incapable of reasoning are obvious exceptions (see Matthew 18:1-10; 19:13,14; 2 Samuel 12:23).

All mankind needs Christianity's unique message from God. To say that the masses, the unreached nations or the heathen are not lost is to deny many clear statements in

Scripture. To answer, How could they be? to the question, Are the heathen lost? may be nothing more than a comfortable, perhaps unconscious way of evading our Lord's last command and great commission: 'Go ye into all the world, and preach the gospel to every creature' (Mark 16:15 AV).

And in practice this is exactly what happens. If a man believes that the heathen are lost, he is much more likely to obey his Lord's command to go to them, making every effort to reach them with living words and loving hands (Ezekiel 3:17; Romans 10:14; Acts 20:24). If he does not believe that they are lost, he has little or no sense of urgency to obey.

Does your sense of justice rebel at the thought of the heathen being lost? Think again. God is the source of your sense of justice. It is derived from his sense of justice, and the stream cannot rise higher than its source. We may be certain that the Judge of all the earth will do right (Genesis 18:25).

If we really believe in Christ and belong to him, his love should constrain us to go and tell of the way of deliverance, life and love. We have no right to keep God's good news to ourselves. Everybody ought to know about his wonderful love.

It was said of the early Moravian missionaries that they saw behind every dark heathen face the yearning face of Christ. Constrained by his love they went forth to tell people everywhere of that love. It is the combined sense of the duty laid upon every Christian by the great commission and the twofold awareness of the love of Christ and the need of the lost that still constrains men and women to make Christ known to those till now unreached.

7
How can I know God's will?

'I wish I knew what I ought to do. I find it so difficult to be sure of God's will.'

Do you ever say things like that? Or do you sometimes think them and keep quiet, because you are afraid of being thought a poor sort of Christian?

The desire to do God's will, no matter how out of step we may be with non-Christians, is one of the hallmarks of a real Christian. Those who are born again want to please their heavenly Father. 'We love him because he first loved us' (1 John 4:19 AV). And love always wants to please the one who is loved. But how can we know what pleases God? How can we get guidance?

Let's be frank about this question of guidance. For some Christians it seems to be the all-important thing in life, whereas what matters, above all else, are forgiveness, a right relationship with God, doing (not just knowing!) his will in our daily lives, sharing fellowship with other Christians, being easy to live with, and bearing faithful witness to Christ by lip and life. By contrast, guidance must be recognised as a relatively small though not unimportant part of life. None the less, there are occasions when big decisions have to be made which will affect the whole course of our lives. At these times we may need special guidance, but most of the time we need to know in more general terms what God's will is for our daily lives. And so we come back to the question, How can we know God's will?

Do you find yourself wishing at times that there was some modern equivalent to the cloud by day and fire by night by which the Israelites were guided through the wilderness? Or something like the mysterious Urim and Thummin ('Lights and Perfections') which Aaron used for solving hard questions, possibly one lighting up for 'Yes' and the other for 'No'?

Life would be simplified for some Christians, they feel, if they had some guidance-giving gadget, or some detailed book of rules. They do want to know God's will, not just in order to know what they ought to do, but so that they can do it intelligently and gladly. They are only too well aware of the command, 'Be ye doers . . . and not hearers only, deceiving your own selves' (James 1:22 AV) The three words missing from the above quotation give us the leading clue to the problem of guidance. 'Be ye doers *of the word.*' It is to God's Word that we must turn if we want to know God's will.

'Yes, I know,' says somebody, 'but I can't find what I'm looking for in the Bible. I get bothered about what books I should be reading, or where I ought to go for my holidays, what clothes I ought to buy or wear, or how to use my spare time and spend my money. I even wish sometimes that somebody would stand over me and tell me what to do each time I have to make a decision.'

You may think I am painting an extreme picture, but there are people who feel like this, and there are some church leaders who encourage such an attitude.

Young children pass through a phase like this in the normal course of their development before they have formed their own judgment of what is appropriate for each occasion.

It is part of the duty of parents to teach them to find the principles that will guide them. For example, in the matter of clothes, 'I thought this was suitable for the occasion' has to replace, 'Mummy said I must wear this.'

The Pharisees had a rule for everything. No less than 1,500 rules governed the Sabbath. Every conceivable situation was covered in the book of rules. All you needed was a good memory, a well-informed friend or patience to work your way through the long list. Then you would know what to do—or wear! But our Lord had no patience with Pharisaism. He substituted relationships for rules and principles for petty regulations. This does not mean there are no rules in Christianity! There are the Ten Commandments and the Sermon on the Mount, for a start. But Christianity is not a legalistic system, a matter of 'Here are the rules to observe; there is a rule for every detail of life, private, corporate, secular and religious; keep the rules and you will be all right.' It is rather a matter of 'Love the Lord first with all your heart and soul and mind and strength, and love your neighbour as yourself. Whatever is consistent with this love is right.'

So instead of asking what the rule is and thumbing through the Bible as if it were a code-book or a handbook of regulations, we must ask what would please the Lord Jesus, and constantly refer to the same book, the Bible, because the answer to the question is there in principle, if not in detail, for every situation. The more familiar we become with the Bible, the more readily shall we discover God's will for our lives at every turn.

I expect most of us have used the phrase 'I felt led . . .' at some time in our life to justify ourselves in some action that is being called in question. Occasionally we have solid ground for making such a statement and, given time, we would be able to produce evidence that justifies us in making such a claim. But more often than not the phrase represents the last feeble refuge of someone who is cornered and knows it, whose pride will not permit him or her to admit an error of judgment, large or small, a minor *faux pas* or a major blunder. 'Don't hold me responsible; blame my guide,' would often be the logical conclusion to 'I felt led,' but few would dare to put it in as many words!

The perils

All guidance is obviously not of God. The Bible takes a very strong line against spiritualist mediums, clairvoyants, palmists and the like. The Word of God does not deny the existence of the occult, or the possibility of guidance emanating from such sources as are blacklisted by Moses in Deuteronomy 18:10-14, but God's people are strictly forbidden to have anything to do with it. We have been warned by God not to be misguided by spiritual influences which are in rebellion against him and his purposes.

But that is negative—'Don't be guided by my enemies.' What about the positive? Can we expect God to indicate to us, 'Now this is what I want you to do'? It depends primarily on who we are. By this I do not mean what sort of temperaments we have, how emotionally stable we are, whether we are psychic or not, but whether we are Christians or not. If we are not Christians—i.e. if we are not in a right relationship with God through trusting in the Lord Jesus Christ as our own personal Saviour—the only guidance we can expect from God will lead us towards repentance and faith in the Saviour. We are hardly entitled to expect his guidance in the everyday affairs of life. My heart is naturally a pocket of resistance against him and his purposes until I trust the Saviour, so that in the minutiae of life I would not particularly wish to be guided by him, unless I were assured that his guidance would make me more comfortable, get me all I wanted, give me a nice, pleasant feeling inside. If, on the other hand, I have trusted myself to the Lord Jesus, I am not my own, I have been bought with a price, and am indebted to him who bought me. I must glorify God, i.e. I must give him the place of honour in my body and in my spirit, in the things I do and the way I do them. This 'must' is gratefully undertaken. 'I love my master . . . and do not want to go free' (Exodus 21:5). To achieve this glorifying of God in what I do and the way I do it, I shall obviously need information as to what does please God. In other words, I need guidance. And guidance has been promised.

God's promises

In both Old and New Testaments we find clear evidence of God's willingness to guide his people. 'I pray thee . . . shew me now thy way,' says Moses. And the Lord replies, 'My presence shall go with thee, and I will give thee rest' (Exodus 33:13,14 AV). There is no promise here of a cut-and-dried blueprint to be hung up in front of Moses, but there is the promise of God's presence for each section of the blueprint, and, by implication, the assurance that there will always be enough of the blueprint visible for Moses to know what steps to take next. The pillar of cloud by day and fire by night were two of the means used to ensure this.

To God the attitude of his people is of great importance, 'The *meek* will he guide in judgment: and the *meek* will he teach his way,' says David (Psalm 25:9 AV), having such assurances from God as, 'I will instruct thee and teach thee in the way which thou shalt go: I will guide thee with mine eye' (Psalm 32:8 AV). Being willing to obey what we already know to be God's will is vital if we would be guided further: 'As thou goest, step by step the way shall open up before thee,' we read in one of the versions of Proverbs 4:12, and 'Thine ears shall hear a word behind thee, saying, This is the way, walk ye in it, when ye turn to the right hand, and when ye turn to the left,' says Isaiah (30:21 AV). And when we cannot see even the next step ahead, God assures us, 'I will bring the blind by a way that they knew not . . . I will make darkness light before them, and crooked things straight' (Isaiah 42:16 AV).

Jesus, the Son of God, amplifies promises like these. He is the Good Shepherd who calls his own sheep by name and leads them out—the Eastern shepherd always going before his sheep. Christ's sheep (Christian believers) follow him, recognising their Shepherd's voice. He goes on to say, 'I am the door: by me if any man enter in, he shall be saved, and shall go in and out, and find pasture . . . My sheep hear my voice, and I know them, and they follow me . . .' (John 10:9,27 AV).

In the record of the Acts of the Apostles we have instance after instance of the risen Lord clearly guiding his people—Peter, Philip, Saul, Ananias, Cornelius, Lydia, and many others. And as Jesus Christ is 'the same yesterday and today', there is in this guidance an implicit promise that he will guide his people in all generations, and therefore he will guide us now. 'This God is our God for ever and ever: he will be our guide even unto [and over and beyond] death' (Psalm 48:14 AV).

The pitfalls
'Have you got any special guidance?' Too many young Christians (and some older ones, too) almost make a fetish

of guidance. They read the promises, they recognise the need for a guided life, they hear of some having extraordinary hunches or being guided in unusual ways, and they begin to think the most wonderful thing in the world is to get similar guidance—the more spectacular the better, of course. 'If I haven't a lurid past, and didn't have a spectacular conversion, at least I can have the limelight that follows some startling guidance, can't I?' We might not openly reason like that, but I am sure that there are subconscious urges from fallen human nature that push us on like this. How differently John the Baptist: 'He must increase, but I must decrease.'

Years ago, when I was at school, many were caught up with the early enthusiasm of the Oxford Group, a movement which emphasised personal guidance. Our school was more partial to Cambridge, and some of the fellows started a Cambridge Group—on similar lines, of course. I was roped in. Every morning we got up earlier (a very good thing) and took our pads and pencils, and let our minds go blank, waiting for God to speak. I wrote down some strange things, but most of what I put was the result of a quickened conscience. Some of what I wrote was thinly disguised wishful thinking. I was 'led' to write to a girl whose athletic prowess I admired. She was not led to reply! My faith in the scheme began to shake. I did not know then the grave dangers that accompany passivity. Those who let their minds go blank do so at their own peril. Some can trace mental, nervous and moral breakdown to this practice. Not all influences that seek to bear down on the human mind are from God. (For example, there are evil spirits that seek to influence us; the Holy Spirit has many adversaries—see 1 John 4:1-6). Nor did I know then how vital it is to bring our minds prayerfully to God's Word first, that he may speak to us and show us his ways and resources as well as our duty. Checking your guidance when you have derived it from other sources is a poor substitute for this.

Some people use the story of Gideon's fleece as a reason for seeking unusual signs at every crossroads of life. There is a grave danger of our deteriorating into machines, substituting levers for personal responsibility. But it is better—and you may think this is a dangerous statement to make, almost encouraging rashness, which is far from its intention—it is better for us to exercise our personal judgment, even if we make a wrong decision, and then face the music, than to shrink into our shells because we cannot feel any all-powerful levers pulling us around anywhere. It is better still, of course, to make the right decision! Human personality is something vastly richer than a bundle of instincts, complexes or reflexes! Rational choice is open to us.

The great realities in the Christian life are God's love for me, as found in Christ, my love for God and my fellow humans, holiness before God, and righteousness in all my dealings with men. 'Guidance' as a phenomenon is not one of the 'top of the agenda' items, but it has become an obsession with far too many whom we look up to as 'very spiritual'. Consequently we find it easy to exaggerate its importance. 'Unless you people see miraculous signs and wonders,' said Jesus to a royal official, 'you will never believe,' a statement which was clearly intended as a rebuke to those listening. And it still contains a rebuke for those who are always clamouring for signs, and don't want to make up their minds until they have stuck a pin in a verse (with their eyes closed, of course), pulled a statement out of a promise-box, read their teacup or counted the number of black cats passed on the way home! 'Sanctified common sense' is the instrument of which the Lord makes most use in directing us in the little things of daily life. A lot of talk about guidance among professing Christians is super-stitious bunkum, the religious equivalent of many a non-Christian's respect for horoscopes! And as I suggested at the beginning of this chapter, 'I felt led . . . ' is often the last resort of someone who hopes to involve higher powers in responsibility and escape the blame for what is all too fre-quently a crass error of judgment, a proof of stubborn prej-udice, or a first-class piece of putting your foot in it. 'Ye that are men, now serve him!' wrote George Duffield in his hymn 'Stand up, stand up for Jesus'. Let us shoulder blame when it is due to us, and make apologies for our ignorance and clumsiness, and not try to wriggle out of our respon-sibility by prefacing our explanation with, 'I felt led . . .', or 'I simply had to . . .', or 'There was no alternative'! Even after the man of Macedonia had been seen by Paul in a vision, a sound judgment had to be formed. Reason and judgment were not bypassed. Common sense had to be exercised. The sign was not sufficient in itself, as a direct appeal to senses or emotions, for Luke, the author of Acts, states that 'we got ready at once, concluding that God had called us to preach the gospel to them' (Acts 16:10).

General principles

In seeking to know the will of God there are certain con-stant principles that we must always bear in mind.

(1) *My will must be bent to God's will* (John 7:17). There must be an honest willingness to do all the will of God, whatever it may mean or cost, wherever it may lead. If in any respect I am not willing, I must be willing to be made willing.

(2) *My mind must be subject to God's mind* (1 Corinthians

2:13; 14:37). There must be a genuine subjection to the revealed will of God as found in the Holy Scriptures. Martin Luther said, 'My conscience is tied to the Word of God.' So must ours be, if we would know his will. I do not need any unusual guidance against cheating ('Thou shalt not steal') or against toying with a deep friendship with an unconverted fellow or girl ('Be ye not unequally yoked together with unbelievers')! One of the fundamental principles of guidance is so simple that it is sometimes overlooked. Nothing forbidden in God's Word can be his will. Ignorance of the Scriptures can result in uncertainty and confusion about what is and what is not the will of God. To know God's will, the most important thing for any Christian, young or old, is to get to know God's Word (Acts 17:11; Psalm 119:11). Regular and systematic Bible-reading will give light, strengthen faith, and help in the making of wise and right decisions.

(3) *I must recognise the limitations of my judgment* (ability to weigh up pros and cons), but I must also recognise that almost all the decisions of my life will be the fruit of using my judgment, counting on God to give me discernment ('The meek will he guide in judgment'), and to overrule if I err in judgment and deviate ('Thine ears shall hear . . . when ye turn to the right or left,' i.e. from the central pathway of the will of God).

Verses 1 and 2 of Romans 12 call for a total surrender to the will of God. If all my property, clothes, etc. are his, I do not need any spectacular guidance about what tie or scarf I should wear (even if I have some spectacular ties or scarves!). I must use my judgment. Unusual guidance will be the most unusual thing. With a foundation of Bible-reading, most of our guidance will come through a will yielded to God, coupled with common sense, i.e. sanctified common sense. As Christians, we don't rush to a rule-book to know what to do each day. We use the common sense God has given us, always ready for him to overrule our decisions in any way he pleases.

(4) *Duty is a clear indication of God's will* (Psalm 15:4b; John 2:5). God's guidance for ordinary things does not come in an extraordinary way. The next duty to be performed is nearly always staring us in the face and is almost certain to be the will of God. That is the way that God guides us. Only very rarely is a Christian honestly ignorant of what really ought to be done next. God's will never conflicts with our plain duty.

The first draft of this chapter was a duty for the day I was writing it. As I was working on it there was a head-on crash outside the house in which I was then living. I did not pray for guidance: I rushed out to see if I could help, and then came back to dial 999. There were no serious casualties, but we had the shaken folk in our home while the police and car experts 'got weaving'. No special guidance was needed. Duty made clear the will of God. The departure of the unexpected guests left me free to return to that duty—a very pleasant one! In a conflict of duties the Christian usually finds one duty raises its head just high enough above others for him to know what to do next.

(5) *Intuitions are not to be treated as infallible*. All are to be tested by God's Word. Occasionally God guides us by 'hunches' and 'intuitions'. One day I was wondering whether I should go seven miles in one direction or three in another. I asked that I might be led in my uncertainty, and had a 'hunch' that I should go the latter way. But most of my 'hunch' was the by-product of reasoning, in which I was asking God to direct me aright. I reached an office in

time to stop a letter which might have altered someone's whole career. I reached a shop in time to talk happily about the Lord with a keen Christian who, soon after my arrival, collapsed and died at my feet. None of his relations was present, and I had to break the news to his wife. I was so glad his grandson had not found him dead on the floor, as this boy was the next to come to the shop. But I very rarely experience guidance such as that. 'Do the next duty to the glory of God and in the power of his Spirit, willing for him to step in if it glorifies him,' is a fair picture of the attitude of most wise Christians to the matter of guidance. Hunches may, or may not, be indication of God's leading. It is better to err on the side of caution, and we must test all hunches by the Word of God. He will never guide us to do anything contrary to his Word.

(6) *Obedience to light we have is a condition of receiving further light upon our pathway.* We cannot expect God to guide us if we are refusing to act on light already given to us. Why should God give us any more light on our pathway if we are not going to do anything about it? 'Do whatever he tells you' (John 2:5). Too many are like the gypsy woman who was seen to toss her twigs into the air three times at a crossroad. 'Why did you throw the twigs up like that?' asked a curious observer. 'To know which way I should go,' answered the woman. 'But why three times?' 'Because it didn't come down the way I wanted to go the other times,' she replied!

(7) *We have no right to insist on being given signs.* Some people always look for unusual signs at every crossroads. There is no indication that this was intended to be the normal practice for all believers. As mentioned earlier, the Lord Jesus rebuked those who sought for signs and wonders. The promises of the Bible are intended to strengthen

our faith, but not to be taken out of their context as 'guidance', and we must be careful not to abuse them.

(8) *Things we are not sure about are not to be treated as matters we can do just what we like with.* For a little while I lived with the Rev. Gerald Gregson in Cambridge. Every morning he looked in the mirror as he put his collar on and recited the formula, 'Now, Gerald, your mother always told you, "If it's doubtful, it's dirty!"' And if it was 'doubtful', into the soiled linen basket it went. Romans 14 teaches us that this illustrates a truly biblical principle. 'When in doubt, don't.' I think it was the saintly R. C. Chapman of Barnstaple who wrote:

The rule that governs my life is this: Anything that dims my vision of Christ, takes away my taste for Bible study, cramps my prayer life, or makes Christian work difficult is wrong for me, and I must as a Christian turn away from it. This simple rule may help you to find a safe path for your feet along life's highway.

Susannah Wesley gave a similar 'simple rule' to John and Charles to put into practice at Oxford—one of the seeds of the Holy Club and the Wesleyan Revival.

We have seen that in the humdrum of everyday life the path of duty walked in to the glory of God is the God-guided path. What about the unusual crises of life, when we are confronted with the choice of a career, or a life-partner, or the next phase in our studies or our work?

(9) *Circumstances are to be viewed as God's framework* (Romans 8:28; Philippians 1:12,13). We need to observe the principles just outlined, and to bear in mind that God is, as Oswald Chambers puts it, 'The Master-Engineer of circumstances'. If I have not contrived to pull these to the shape of

my choosing, and an inward sense of rest or general sense of the rightness of things points in the same direction, I may be fully confident of being in the will of God. Then we—you and I—may move forward, counting on him to check us if in any way we have misread the evidence or misinterpreted his Word or our own convictions.

(10) *Older Christian friends are not to be ignored* simply because 'they belong to another generation', nor are they to be followed slavishly simply because they are more experienced than we are. We do well to heed the advice of godly friends who have passed our way. They are not automatically 'wrong' because they were born so long ago or are beginning to go grey! They may save us from wasting hours of our time, even years of our life.

Extraordinary situations call for special prayer, and perhaps a day or two quietly away to get things in perspective and possibly to receive unusual guidance. The advice of older Christians will often help us, and we should be neither too proud to seek it nor too dependent on it.

(11) *Christian biographies may be read with keen interest and great profit.* From them we may learn much about how God handles his people and guides them in his 'providential way'.

(12) *Don't be in a hurry.* Remembering that the Lord Jesus spent a night in prayer before choosing his disciples, some of us may find it really helpful to spend an unhurried season of prayer in a quiet place, seeking to have a clear mind and an unwarped judgment as we decide on our career. But for many of us the processes that lead to this decision are so slow and sure that such a time seeking guidance would be quite uncalled for. We might instead use such hours for self-dedication to the vocation he has revealed to us.

A God-guided life is lived on a daily basis in quiet humility, without fanaticism or exhibitionism. 'Behold, thy servants are ready to do whatsoever my lord the king shall appoint' (2 Samuel 15:15 AV). 'Whatsoever he saith unto you, do it' (John 2:5 AV). Each Christian reader can prove that 'the path of the just is as the shining light, that shineth more and more unto the perfect day' (Proverbs 4:18 AV).

8
Do you really pray?

If you were asked what you think is the greatest need among Christians today, I wonder what you would say. Would you say we need a greater sense of urgency and an awareness that we are passing through a time of great crisis?

Many feel that the only hope for Britain and the world is a true spiritual revival. Surely this is true. But if you are a born-again believer in the Lord Jesus Christ, I am sure you will probably agree with me when I say that the greatest immediate need among the children of God is the deepening of the prayer-life. If there is one thing more than another that the devil attacks and seeks to suppress, and even extinguish, it is our communion with God.

Every born-again believer has to confess that this is his or her weakest point. We believe in prayer, we agree that prayer is important, we talk, perhaps too glibly, about answers to prayer, and yet our prayer-life is superficial, hurried and often selfish. If we truly belong to Christ and have prayed the opening prayer of the Christian life, 'God be merciful to me a sinner', then within our hearts is a longing to know more of prayer, both personally and in fellowship with other believers.

Do you long to know God better? Do you long to see his power at work, in answer to prayer, in the lives of those around you? Then you must pray! Has your prayer-life nearly dried up? Or has it never really got going?

I want to share with you some thoughts on this wonderful, yet difficult, subject of prayer. I use the word 'difficult' advisedly. I have yet to meet the Christian who always finds prayer easy or is satisfied with the way he prays or the length of time he spends in prayer. Don't you find that Christians who talk about the subject at all are ashamed of the poverty of their prayer-life?

On the other hand, you may know someone who seems to breathe the very atmosphere of prayer. Don't you wish you were like that, without hypocrisy or spiritual pride? The Lord is the same in his attitude to all who call upon him, but it takes time and experience to become a person whose whole life is soaked in prayer.

If you don't think that prayer is really important, you will never make time for it. And nobody knows but God and you how much time you could give to prayer—time that at present is given to other things. No matter how good those other things are, that time is wasted if you should be praying. There are a few people who give time to prayer when they should be sharing the responsibility of household duties, but such people are very few and far between!

What is prayer?

Prayer is speaking to the living God from the heart. It is personal companionship with him, and it is one of the greatest privileges open to everyone who has been born again through personal faith in Christ. Many Christians feel they can pray only in their own words. Others can use other people's scriptural prayers just as much 'from the heart', like many of those the Reformers handed on to us in the *Book of Common Prayer*. Think, for example, of that lovely collect beginning with, 'Almighty God, unto whom all hearts are open, all desires known, and from whom no secrets are hid . . .'

The Bible gives us different aspects of prayer for our example. Adoration is prayer, confession to God is prayer, thanksgiving is prayer, but lots of Christians find their prayer-time is so overcrowded with petition that thanksgiving has been crowded out. Why not make a list of all the things you have to thank God for and go through it on your knees by your bed tonight or in some quiet place at any time?

Supplication is prayer, but God is not a kind of Omnipotent Supervisor of a spiritual supermarket who will provide anything Christians ask for! He is our heavenly Father to whom we come in love and trust, with a desire to know him better.

Prayer is a Christian duty

Prayer is not an optional extra for very keen Christians. Our Lord says that his disciples 'should always pray and not give up'. His life is a wonderful example of this. He gave the first part of his days on earth to communion with his Father in heaven (see Mark 1:35). Sometimes he had prolonged times of prayer when great decisions were to be made (see Luke 6:12). His High Priestly prayer recorded in John 17 gives us an amazing insight into his praying. That same evening in the Garden of Gethsemane, the veil is lifted yet again upon his praying, taking us to the very heart of prayer (Matthew 26:36-44). We learn from our Lord's praying there that the main purpose of prayer is not to get God on our side, for our comfort, but to put ourselves at his disposal for his will to be done in us and through us, at any cost. What we *want* and what God *wills* for us are often not identical. Nothing could be plainer in Jesus' prayer: 'My Father, if it is possible, may this cup be taken from me. Yet not as I will, but as you will' (Matthew 26:39,42,44).

'We perish if we cease from prayer', runs James Montgomery's hymn. Prayer is like a pipeline under the ocean of materialism and indifference and unbelief. The apostles prayed. And when they prayed, things happened! The power of the Spirit fell in strengthening power in answer to their prayers. When they were persecuted for their faith they didn't pray for safety but for boldness to go on speaking God's Word. Some missionaries wrote from Africa at the time of the Mau Mau troubles, asking prayer for Christians there, Africans and Europeans alike, 'not that we may be kept safe but that we may be kept faithful'.

Somebody once said to Archbishop Temple, 'I can't understand a man with your education praying. Why do you do it?' The answer was simple. 'Because things happen when I pray which do not happen if I do not pray.' And there is a more vital answer still: it is God's will that we should seek his face. In his mercy he deigns to use the prayers of forgiven sinners for the blessing of other lives.

Nothing is too great or too trivial to bring to God in prayer. More things are still wrought by prayer than this world dreams of, for when the hand that moves the world moves us to pray, 'prayer moves the hand that moves the world'.

Read again the words of our Lord Jesus: 'If ye then, being evil, know how to give good gifts unto your children: how much more shall your heavenly Father give the Holy Spirit to them that ask him?' (Luke 11:13). When did you last take this verse seriously?

If you find your thoughts wander when you pray, why

81

not compile a prayer-list of people and situations that you know, and use it systematically? It often helps, too, to pray about the subject to which your thoughts have wandered. Everyone finds difficulties in prayer, but these can be overcome if we are prepared to face them in the strength of the Lord. Where there's a will, there's a way. May God give us the will!

Praying with others
It is a sad commentary on the condition of the Christian church today that Christians can meet in each other's homes without having any prayer together or even talking of the things of the Lord, and yet speak of having had 'a time of happy fellowship together'!

What sort of fellowship is it where there is no prayer? We may automatically make time for a meal or a snack when we meet our Christian friends, but time for prayer involves effort and determination. Will you make time for prayer whenever you meet your Christian friends? And will you make sure your prayer is not a quick apology to the Lord for having discussed absent people in a way that would have shocked unbelievers with decent standards of loyalty, let alone grieved the spirit of love?

It has warmed my heart to know of small groups (generally housewives) who meet together regularly in a home to pray. Have you thought of asking some Christian neighbours, who find it hard to get to the church prayer-meeting, to meet with you in your home to pray, perhaps once a fortnight or once a month?

Most Christians find it very hard to pray aloud for the first time, but each time they make the effort it becomes easier. A prayer-meeting is much more inspiring if those who come to it are prepared to pray aloud, even if there is not always time for them all to do so. If you would like to take a helpful audible part in a prayer-meeting, here are some hints.

- Pray about the prayer-meeting before you get there. Inform your mind. Decide what you are going to pray about. Focus your mind. Pray for one thing at a time. Don't hesitate to pray briefly more than once in a prayer-meeting, or to pray in more detail for something that someone else has prayed about in general.

- Speak naturally. Don't cultivate a special voice for praying or use a special vocabulary. Never pray *at* people present. That is an abuse of the privilege of a prayer-meeting. Praying *for* them is a different matter! If you are very nervous, breathe deeply several times before you pray. This helps you to relax.

- Don't be afraid of hearing your own voice, on the one hand, and don't pray in order to hear it or to impress other Christians, on the other. If someone with a stronger voice than yours starts praying at the same moment as you, wait until they finish, and then pray after them. The others will be waiting for you to do so.

- Pray *short prayers* in an open prayer-meeting. Nothing kills the spirit of a prayer-meeting more than long, rambling prayers. This may not apply in a specialised prayer-meeting, where time is unlimited and it is understood that the few present will pray for as long as they like. But in a regular prayer-meeting, where there are more than two or three people present, with several ready to pray after us, long prayers can be a subtle form of selfishness and can stop young Christians from ever opening their mouths.

'Lord, teach us to pray.'

9
What is 'praying in the Spirit'?

How should we react when we are accused of 'not praying in the Spirit'? A mature Christian lady I know was very worried that she seemed to be missing out because she had not received 'the gift of tongues'. Someone explained to her it was simply a matter of letting her tongue go and making baby noises, and in time she would acquire increasing fluency and ability to produce sounds which would be a meaningful language to the ears of angels. Her well-instructed biblical mind knew this was not 'praying in the Spirit', but no one explained to her what 'praying in the Spirit' really was.

'Praying in the Spirit': how should we understand these words? Is it a practice limited to those who claim to pray in tongues, or does it have a much deeper meaning that is experienced by every Christian?

It is very important to understand the meaning of this phrase, because twice in Scripture we are told to do this very thing. In Ephesians 6:10-17 Paul gives instructions to his readers. But before the expression to 'pray in the Spirit' comes the instruction to 'put on the full armour of God' so that we may be fully prepared and able to stand our ground in the fight against the devil and his armies. This armour consists of various spiritual characteristics that are pictured as being part of a soldier's uniform: the 'belt of truth'; the 'breastplate of righteousness'; 'the shield of faith with which you can extinguish all the flaming arrows of the evil one'; the 'helmet of salvation' and the 'sword of the Spirit', which is the word of God'. We are told in Hebrews 4:12 that this 'sword of the Spirit' is 'sharper than any double-edged sword' that a soldier may carry; 'it penetrates even to dividing soul and spirit, joints and marrow; it judges the thoughts and attitudes of the heart.' Only after we have read the Word of God or 'the sword of the Spirit' and applied it to our hearts and lives, are we told to 'pray in the Spirit'.

We are then given a list of instructions about what 'praying in the Spirit' entails. This activity is not something mystical that divides believers, but prayer that is inspired by the Word of God and is commanded for all Christians. Who is to be prayed for?—the saints; when are we to pray?—on all occasions; what form should our prayers take?—they should be all kinds of prayers and requests. Thus we observe that praying in the Spirit is believers praying for fellow believers as well as for the lost.

In Jude verse 20 we are also told to pray in the Spirit. Paul has already warned us in Ephesians 6 that the way to beat the devil is to make sure we are steeped in the Word of God. Here in Jude, the brother of James warns us not about the devil but about scoffers. These are unbelievers, devoid of the Spirit of God, who make mischief by trying to divide believers against each other. We combat such people by building ourselves up in our most holy faith, especially by reading and studying the Word of God. We also fight such people by 'praying in the Spirit', or praying as the Word of God commands. Again this is nothing mystical or even a special ability that is only given to a small band of Christians. It is a command of our Lord, in his Word, for all believers.

Praying in the Spirit means we are only to pray for those things which Scripture allows. This does not mean that the Holy Spirit only speaks to us when we are reading the Bible. There are times a person or a situation is put into our mind at moments during the day or night. If someone suddenly comes to mind or we have a burden for a particular situation, this is a good prompting to take that person or situation before the Lord in prayer. Indeed, we may feel compelled to pray, and this may be attributed to the leading of the Holy Spirit. Everything we pray for should be within the scope of Scripture. This is not to say that we cannot be specific in prayers, nor that we must use Bible language and pattern on every occasion—though this is a good practice. It does mean that we approach God in the way we are shown in the many scriptural examples of prayer that we have, and that we pray for those things which would honour the Lord and accord with his revealed will for his people. It is in Scripture that we see the mind of Christ, and the Bible should condition our approach to God through Christ our mediator.

Do Christians always pray in the Spirit?

Does this mean that every time a Christian prays, he or she 'prays in the Spirit'?

In one way it would appear to be so, for we are told in Romans 8:9 that every Christian is 'prompted' 'not by the sinful nature but by the Spirit . . . And if anyone does not have the Spirit of Christ, he does not belong to Christ'. The Spirit of Christ indwells all believers, living and working in their hearts and lives, prompting and guiding them. If the Spirit is not in a person's life, then that person is not a believer.

However, although we have said this, Ephesians 6:18

does exhort us, 'And pray in the Spirit on all occasions', as if it is possible for believers not always to do so. The prayers of believers are constantly being influenced by fleshly and worldly thoughts. It may be said that when these thoughts take hold we are not 'praying in the Spirit' in its full meaning.

In our private devotions there are a hundred and one things that may enter our minds as we come to the Lord in prayer. Even legitimate duties can crowd in upon us as we seek the face of the Lord. We must always be on our guard against this happening and try to find a suitable time, even for a short while, to be alone with our Lord. At public prayer meetings or church services our minds can wander, especially if we are tired or stressed. We find it difficult to concentrate. There is also a danger, perhaps even a greater danger, of 'fleshly influences' coming upon those who lead public prayers. There are those who like to hear the sound of their own voices. They may be very articulate or feel it is their duty always to pray in public. There are those who have been told by others they have the gift of prayer and pride has become inflated in their hearts.

Christians must always be on guard against such 'worldly' and 'fleshly' influences invading their prayers. When it does happen, however—and it will from time to time—it does not mean in any way that the Spirit of God has left us. This abandonment cannot happen to a true believer. The Holy Spirit may be 'grieved' (Ephesians 4:30), but he does not forsake those whose lives have been sealed for the day of redemption.

Whether in public or private, our prayers are often weak, limited, poorly expressed or even arrogant; for though we are indwelt by the Spirit, we are still human, with all our failings and imperfections. Words can come out all wrong or we cannot express our feelings. It is so reassuring to know that

> In the same way, the Spirit helps us in our weakness. We do not know what we ought to pray for, but the Spirit himself intercedes for us with groans that words cannot express. And he who searches our hearts knows the mind of the Spirit, because the Spirit intercedes for the saints in accordance with God's will (Romans 8:26-27).

A weak prayer, yes; perhaps even a misguided prayer; but a prayer heard by God because of the work of the Holy Spirit—his meaningful intercession turning our groans into responsible intercession for others.

Praying 'out of the Spirit'

Although there can so often be fleshly influences that hinder the prayers of believers, it would seem that it is only unbelievers who will truly 'pray in the flesh' or 'pray outside the Spirit', for they do not have the Spirit of God dwelling in them. There is a warning in Matthew 6 that there are unbelievers who obtain some satisfaction from praying at a church meeting or on the street corner, even though they do not mean the words they say. Our Lord calls them 'hypocrites' (v.5). They appear to enjoy the accolade of those who hear them. It is very important, however, to remember that although we may say these people are praying, they are not actually speaking with God. They are speaking to the air, to the walls, or to the people around them. They are accused by the Lord of 'babbling' and using many words. It is after this warning that the Lord gives us an example of what prayer should be like, commonly called 'The Lord's Prayer' and recorded for us in verses 9-14.

In summary, we have seen that to pray in the Spirit does not mean to pray in tongues. Neither is it a gift of prayer limited to those believers who claim to have it. All believers pray in the Spirit, for all believers have the Spirit of God living in their hearts and lives. However, a spirit of worldliness can come into the hearts of believers and manifest itself in our prayers. We must always be on our guard against this, recognise it for what it is, and pray for help to deal with it. Those who lead public prayer may have to fight against this most of all. However, even weak, faltering, or wrongly motivated prayers of believers are heard by God because of the work of our Lord on the cross and the fact that the Holy Spirit dwells in believers' hearts. It is only those who 'pray' as unbelievers who truly 'pray in the flesh' or 'out of the Spirit'. It is these people who desperately need the work of the Holy Spirit in their lives so that they may know the peace of God in their lives. Only then will their prayers become acceptable to God.

10
Dare you be different?

Don't be fooled. Don't let anyone deceive you by what he writes, declares or suggests. 'No immoral, or greedy person—such a man is an idolator—has any inheritance in the kingdom of Christ and of God' (Ephesians 5:5).

Satan deceived Eve with 'vain words' and empty promises. Satan can never give the rich fulfilment he promises. But he has been using the same tactics with people ever since—not without considerable success. Those false teachers in early church history who were known as Gnostics taught that what you did with your body didn't affect your soul. There seem to be traces of a modern form of Gnosticism in some contemporary religious books, which suggest that, so long as they have some 'therapeutic value', sexual relationships outside the marriage bond need not necessarily be sinful, and might even bring some spiritual release. When a bishop says that in 99, or even 100, cases out of 100, sex relations before marriage may be wrong, but not intrinsically so, it becomes far too easy for people to soothe their conscience by arguing that their particular situation is the exception that proves the rule, and flatter themselves by insisting that they are 'not being promiscuous, so it's not nearly as bad as . . .'

Let us not be deceived by plausible talk. We can all find reasons for doing what we want to do but know to be wrong! Ephesians 5:6 reads, 'Because of such things [listed in verses 3-5] God's wrath comes [even now] on those who are disobedient', i.e. those who flout God's laws and disregard his authority. Make no mistake about it: those who indulge in such sins and never come to repentance and life in Christ, will surely experience God's wrath, his righteous indignation against sin, and his active punishment of sin (v.6) both in this life (Romans 1:18-32) and the next (Revelation 20:10-15). There is hope and cleansing for a man who turns from these sins to Christ (1 Corinthians 6:9-11). But there is no hope and no purging in this life or the next for the man who persistently prefers these things to Christ (Hebrews 10:26-30; Revelation 22:11).

Dare to be different

Christ gave himself up for us in self-sacrifice and he calls us to walk in love (Ephesians 5:2). Love does not mean self-indulgence. Sexual adventures are 'out' for the Christian (v.3). Fornication covers any sexual experience between people not married to one another. We must not confuse the idea of true love with any indulgence in what God has forbidden. The 'new morality' popularised in *Honest to God* and elsewhere goes seriously astray in this respect. God has placed the boundaries of the marriage relationship around sexual experience. These boundaries cannot be crossed with God's blessing. But in some parts of the world the clock is being put back to the times of the 'old immorality'. The *Expositor's Greek Testament* says:

> The moral life of the Graeco-Roman world had sunk so low that, while protests against the prevailing corruption were never entirely lacking, fornication had long come to be regarded as a matter of moral indifference, and was indulged in without shame or scruple not only by the

91

masses but by philosophers and men of distinction who otherwise led exemplary lives.

All uncleanliness, whether of thought, imagination, desire, word or deed, literature, photographs, videos, or any other form, is ruled out for the Christian. So is covetousness, whether we understand this as referring to the inordinately strong desire to possess things or the strong desire to possess people, i.e. lust, whether natural or unnatural. As Christians it is our solemn duty to fight against the uprising from sinful fallen nature of such desires, stirred up as they are by massive persistent modern propaganda. Each of us must have our own spiritual 'underground resistance movement'. What is more, these things are not fit subjects for discussion among Christians (v.3), who are set apart ('God's holy people') to do God's will in a world in revolt against his claims and his standards. Christian workers may have to hear 'confessions' from people sinfully involved, but such are not for repetition in ordinary conversation.

Obscenity (v.4), vulgar or indecent language and foolish conversation, talking a lot of nonsense or talking for talking's sake are 'out' also. A clean sense of humour is a great asset to a hard-pressed Christian. The jesting which is outlawed for Christians is not inoffensive, innocent fun, but that jesting which is 'out of place', i.e. not consistent with professing to belong to the Lord Jesus Christ. Smutty stories, suggestive talking, borderline wit are ruled out for Christians. We must turn away, for example, from the vulgar humour of many a seaside postcard. We must not cultivate the kind of humour which is facetious about everything, which turns everything into a huge joke and is always trying to raise a laugh with clever talk. Our cheerfulness is to be linked with the Spirit's working within our hearts and not with our own natural subtlety. Someone has said, 'Christians must take life seriously, but not always solemnly.'

'Have nothing to do with the fruitless deeds of darkness, but rather expose them' (v.11). A girl who works in a factory has explained to me that because she is part of a group working as a single unit in this factory she cannot walk away when a smutty story is being told. Instead she concentrates on a verse of Scripture. She does not share the vulgar humour and she silently rebukes it. The quality of our life is a much better rebuke than words of condemnation, though there are times when we should speak. After Christ's name has been used in vain, a Christian has sometimes said quietly, 'If only you knew Christ personally you wouldn't use his name so lightly', or just 'I wish you really knew him.' Suggestive pin-ups and 'daring' dresses are not for Christians. Some of the clothes worn these days make me sorry for the young men of today, surrounded by the constant pressure of propaganda which suggest the only thing worth living for is sex.

Christian girls, don't lower your standards to 'get your man'; God wants your man to be his man, and a man of God won't be attracted to a girl who tries to make herself 'attractive' by lowering her standards. Dare to leave your future in God's hands!. Trust him to give you the life-partner of his choice or to give you a satisfying life of service without a life-partner. Far better to be single in God's will than married out of it! Beware of the charming young man who invites you to his bedsitter, even if it is 'to discuss religious matters'. Better to be safe than sorry. It is not usually the promiscuous women who find themselves in trouble with an unwanted baby, but the girls who are ignorant and too readily trusting.

Christian boys, don't lower your standards because you want to appear 'big'. If you are worth your place in a team, for instance, and are in God's will, you will keep it without any compromise or attempt to gain popularity. An ounce of respect is worth a pound of popularity. This has been proved by friends of mine at international level as well as in local sport. Turning back from sport to boy-girl friendships, if you really respect the girl you are fond of, you will be determined at all costs to keep for marriage the precious things God has designed for marriage. And if you really trust the Lord Jesus, you will remember to ask, What would please him? instead of, What can I get away with? And you will seek to do his will out of gratitude to him who gave his life out of love for us.

Be prepared to resist peer pressure

Peer pressure, that is, the pressure of values and behaviour which are today taken for granted, is a marked feature of our media-influenced society. It is taken for granted that it is right to seek pleasure as an end in itself and to conform to the expectations of our peers. The Epicurean philosophy —eat, drink and be merry, for tomorrow we die—is all around us. It is like an irresistible tide that carries all before it.

What should you do about it? First, you should uncover its false values. 'Tomorrow we die' is true, but after death comes judgment (Hebrews 9:27), a truth suppressed now but one which will have to be acknowledged one day. As Christians you and I are to discern the false values of our society for what they are—lies and deceptions. We are to *think* with renewed minds which are able 'to test and approve what God's will is' (Romans 12:2).

Having uncovered the false values which dominate life

today you must be prepared to swim against the tide. You must not allow fear of others to determine how you live. You must make it your business to fear God, and then you will not fear men. You may be ridiculed and abused for the stand you take—but if you would please God you cannot give in to the pressure exerted by the godless. Take heart from God's Word: 'Blessed is the man who does not walk in the counsel of the wicked or stand in the way of sinners or sit in the seat of mockers. But his delight is in the law of the LORD, and on his law he meditates day and night' (Psalm 1:1-2).

Demonstrate your faith

God has called his children to be children of light, in contrast to the darkness around them, in which they themselves previously lived (Ephesians 5:8). They are to show forth the fruit of his Spirit in positive goodness, in sincerity of life and truthfulness of speech (v.9). God is no man's debtor. Those who turn from the sins mentioned in this chapter have their reward in this life as well as in heaven. They have peace of mind and conscience. Their personal relationships are free from the pangs of remorse. The light of their personal relationships shines before men and glorifies their Father who is in heaven. And one day they will hear these wonderful words, 'Well done, good and faithful servant! . . . Come and share your master's happiness!' (Matthew 25:23).

Dare to be different! But to do so you will need the backbone of Daniel (see Daniel 1:8), the courage of Paul (see Acts 24:25), and the vision of Stephen (see Acts 7:55-56).

11
How may you be a useful Christian?

How can I be a useful Christian? How can I help people? I do so want to be used.' This was said to me once by a student who had not been a Christian very long. God had already burdened his heart. He knew that he had only one life here on earth and that it would soon be over. He also knew that only work done for the Lord is work that will really last. This young man also knew that God had chosen him to be saved and that he was 'to bear fruit to God' (Romans 7:4). He wanted his life to bear witness to the Lord Jesus. He was not content to be known only as a man with recently acquired strong religious convictions. He wanted to be used by God to bring sinners to a saving knowledge of his Son. He wanted also to help Christians know God better. All this he wanted with a heartfelt desire.

Do you have similar longings? These longings should be in every Christian's heart because the Father is glorified when we bear much fruit. In this way we are also easily identifiable as real disciples of the Lord Jesus Christ (John 15:8).

Our motives matter!
We must constantly examine our hearts to see what our motives for serving the Lord Jesus really are. We cannot expect God to use us if what is really important to us is our

reputation and what others think about us. We may have great zeal or keenness, or always want to do things better than anyone else. We must be very careful to examine our true motives. Do we really just want everyone to think that we are 'the best'? Our aim must be that God's is the name we glorify, not our own. We must do everything properly and to the best of our ability so that the Lord Jesus shines through us, but it is in his name that we do things, not ours. In 2 Thessalonians 1:12 Paul says, 'We pray this so that the name of the Lord Jesus may be glorified in you, and you in him, according to the grace of God and the Lord Jesus Christ.'

Our human inadequacy

But it is not only actions that can have a dubious motive; words can as well. We may have been given the ability to 'have a way with words'. We find it easy to talk to people and they to us. We may tell someone the wonderful truth that Christ died for our sins. They may see that truth for themselves and be wonderfully converted. Yet we know that it is nothing we can do or say that makes people Christians. That is a work of the Father alone. We are told in John 6:44, 'No-one can come to me unless the Father who sent me draws him . . .' No clever argument of ours or anybody else's, no human pressure can bring people to Christ. We may by our pressure produce some sort of decision, but that does not make a person a Christian.

Our longing must be not just that someone has been truly converted, wonderful though that event is, but that the Saviour shall see the travail of his soul and be satisfied. If the Lord should have used us, we must resist the feeling that our reputation has been enhanced by our being the instrument in another's conversion. Our gifts must never hide the giver. We cannot do God's work in our own strength or in our own way. We are not adequate when left to ourselves. Our sufficiency comes from God alone. Only he can make us fit for his service. And God, wonderful to relate, is pleased to work through us, weak and sinful though we are. We are told in 2 Corinthians 12:9,19, 'My grace is sufficient for you, for my power is made perfect in weakness . . . That is why, for Christ's sake, I delight in weakness.' May God purify our motives until his glory is our chief concern (1 Peter 4:10,11).

Full surrender
If we really want the Lord to use us, we must make sure he has all there is of us. If your friend lets you use his or her car for a journey, they do not remove the spare wheel, still less any of the vital working parts. Your friend would let you have all of it. How can we expect the Lord to use us if we keep back from him bits and pieces of our lives? Are we really not saying to him that we are the real 'boss'? that we are the ones who decide how much he can have? Instead we should be gladly proclaiming, either by our lives or by our lips, that 'Christ is the master of my fate, Christ is the captain of my soul.' 'You are not your own; you were bought at a price' (1 Corinthians 6:20). Let us gladly then give God the place of honour in our body and in our spirit, for both belong rightly to him. He paid for our person, not just for our pardon. Christ is both our Lord and our King. Some try to separate the two aspects. They accept that Christ died for their sins, but they do not accept that he has the right to rule over them. But our lives cannot be divided like this. It obviously gives God great joy to use his servants who are completely at his disposal. Remember that when we give our lives totally to God, he is a perfect

timekeeper. He will put us in the right place at the right time. May we have the joy that comes with being used in this way!

Faith in God's promises
Some of God's people have made solemn vows or promises to him when dedicating their lives to him. But the vows we make to God are not nearly so important as the promises he makes to us, his children. In Matthew 4:19 and Mark 1:17 the Saviour said, '. . . I will make you fishers of men.' This held good for his first disciples, those Galilean fishermen. It was said in language they could understand. He promised to make them 'fishers of men', and this he did. But this same promise holds good for us today. His invitation is for salvation and for service. The word 'service' may sound very daunting, but his service is perfect freedom. What I offer, God takes. What he takes, he cleanses. Who would offer a guest a dirty cup and expect them to use it immediately? The cup would have to be washed first. What God cleanses, he fills. What he fills, he uses. The life we live should be nothing less than the life of Christ living in us through the Holy Spirit. Paul tells us in Romans 12:1 to 'offer your bodies as living sacrifices, holy and pleasing to God—which is your spiritual worship'. As we have already seen, we cannot divide Christ as Saviour and as King. Neither can we divide what we believe and what we do as Christians. What we do is an outward expression of what we believe.

We must not let the world squeeze us into its mould. Materialism is all around us and it is so easy to be sucked in by it and its values. It is only when our minds are being renewed by the daily intake of Scripture and by communion with our Lord that we can prove how good, acceptable and perfect God's will is for our lives. We may well ask, What right have I to keep anything back from the hands that were wounded to save me? When we give him our lives we know they are in safe hands. But we must also know that when we keep back part or all of our lives from him, we are at great risk. In Matthew 10:34-42 the Lord warns us what will happen to those who put anything or anyone before him. But he ends with the glorious words, 'I tell you the truth, he will certainly not lose his reward.' The Lord indeed is no man's debtor.

Daily yielding

But despite the Lord's great promises in Scripture, many believers are still afraid of some great crises that will come upon them when they put all they have and all they are at his disposal. It could be said that that way of thinking is only natural. Handing over our lives does not come easily to our human nature. But remember, the first act of conscious, full surrender is only the beginning. Think of the vows taken in all sincerity on a wedding day. Important as those vows may be, we cannot rest on them. It is hard work to make a marriage harmonious. Solemn vows do not guarantee daily harmony and co-operation. It takes a real effort to understand each other and to find out what our partner is really like. It does not come in a week, or a month, or a year. It takes both time and effort.

Perhaps the analogy falls short here, because in a marriage both partners have to work hard to make it work. In the relationship we have with God, his ways are perfect and therefore do not need changing. It is *our* ways that need constant adjustment. We need to put ourselves afresh into his hands each day, so that he may cleanse us from the defilement that comes through contact with a rebellious, fallen world. We also need cleansing from the defilement that springs up in our own hearts. We must come to him daily, for we cannot expect to be used by him daily unless we do so. Remember the 'three Ds'—daily dogged discipline.

Hard work
Do you ever say, 'I can never find the verse I am looking for in my Bible'? God cannot be expected to do for us what we can do for ourselves. If we are to be used by God in helping others in spiritual things, we must know our way through our Bible. The secret of this, as with so many other things, is practice, practice, practice. We can never excel at anything, be it music, sport or handicrafts, without lots of practice. Serious Bible study is called for as well as devotional Bible reading. We must be like the Bereans in Acts 17:11-12 who 'received the message with great eagerness and examined the Scriptures every day to see if what Paul said was true'. When we have heard someone speak or preach, we should go back over the passage when we get home and see if what was said was right. It does not mean we are to be 'picky' or critical. We are not to grumble to others about the content of the delivery or the message the sermon contained. With the help of the Holy Spirit we are to be constantly on our guard that we keep to the truth of Scripture so that the devil may not gain a hold. We are warned in 2 Timothy 1:14, 'Guard the good deposit that was entrusted to you'. We are to be good workmen, rightly handling the word of truth (2 Timothy 2:15).

The importance of prayer
There are so many in need around us that we want our lives to be a blessing to at least some of them in some way.

But we know we cannot touch every life—we are not God and do not have infinite resources. When Maurice Wood was made Bishop of Norwich, he asked his friends to pray with him,

All through this day, O Lord, let me touch as many lives as possible for thee. Every life I touch, do thou by thy Holy Spirit quicken, whether the word I speak, the prayer I pray or the life I live. In the name of the Lord Jesus. Amen.

That is a truly commendable prayer. But there are certain individuals God wants us to help in a particular way. So our prayers should also include asking God to show us the areas where we should be concentrating. We can touch individual lives both in the words we say and in the acts we do. We have already touched on this in the subject of bringing others to Christ. Here I want to concentrate on praying for others. If you are a believer, do you remember how you heard the gospel of Christ? It was probably through personal contact, maybe at school, college, work or club. The Lord can lead someone to talk to you at a particular time, in a particular place. We must be constantly praying that the Lord will use us in a similar manner. As someone else has put it,

Lord, lay some soul upon my heart,
And love that soul through me;
And may I humbly do my part,
To win that soul to thee.

Christ himself is the great soul-winner. We are his auxiliaries, his servants. May we not get in his way, either by overactivity or unavailability. We need heavenly wisdom to know when to speak and when to be silent. There is a right moment for everything. Satan will do his utmost either to fill us with self-importance or with fear of man. It may take years to recover from somebody's wrong approach or failure to seize a God-given opportunity. We know that no one will be kept out of the kingdom by our failure. In the end the great Shepherd is going to get all his sheep safely home: 'When he has brought out all his own . . .' (John 10:4). This promise is a great comfort, but it must not be an excuse for us to think, 'If God has everything under control, then if we fail to seize the moment, there will always be someone else to speak about the Lord.' The Lord has work for us to do.

D. L. Moody, the famous American evangelist, said, 'The way to reach the masses [with the gospel] is to reach them one by one.' This is similar to C. H. Spurgeon's comment, 'The best fruit is hand-plucked' (we must be careful here not to imply that one soul is of more value than another). May I ask for whose conversion you are praying? Or have you given up praying for conversions because the response has been so slow in coming and you have concluded that those you were praying for cannot be among God's elect? Remember, God is not impressed by our modern 'instant' culture. He is not in a hurry. 'With the Lord a day is like a thousand years, and a thousand years are like a day' (2 Peter 3:8). When we hear of someone turning to Christ in true repentance and faith, it nearly always transpires that someone, somewhere, had been praying fervently for that particular individual. George Müller, known for his orphanage in Bristol, prayed for someone he was at school with. He prayed sixty years for this man who only turned to Christ after Müller's death. Pray on.

We are challenged to pray for those in authority over us in our land. Was there ever a greater need for such prayer? Our political leaders are trying to get back to basics while ignoring or denying the most basic need of all, namely, for men and women to get right with God. There are so many instances of prayer in the New Testament. We see over and over again that God listens to the prayers of his people. If it is he who moves them to pray, how could it be otherwise? Prayer is the power that makes preaching effective. The prayer meeting has been called 'the power-house of the church'. No prayer, no power. We must make every effort to be there; it is not a meeting we can say is 'not for us'. When the church changes its prayer meeting so that prayer is squeezed to the sidelines, it is on a slippery slope. By our prayers we can reach into countries where open missionary work is banned. By our prayers we can put up a shield against the efforts of godless men to capture Britain for their own purposes. Again—pray on.

Holy living
'The greatest need of my people is my personal holiness', said that saintly Dundee minister, Robert Murray M'Cheyne, who was called into the presence of his Lord whom he served so well at the early age of twenty-nine years. He, being dead, yet speaks. His influence has been far-reaching. His words, his actions, his faithfulness, his complete lack of jealousy and self-importance still challenge young people today. It is said that actions speak louder than words. We must back up with consistent lives what we say with our lips. But we must be constantly on our guard to shun everything that suggests an 'I am holier than you' approach. We tread a very fine line here and it is something we can only achieve with the help of the Holy Spirit.

Kindness, unselfishness, cheerfulness at all times, an outgoing interest in other people, their problems and difficulties—these are some of the qualities that impress believers and make them more willing to listen to what we have to say. Those whose lives are fragrant with Christ, because they are meeting with him in the Bible every day, earn the right to speak to people who might otherwise be untouchable. It was the radiance of a Dublin solicitor that was one of the most powerful influences over my development as a teenage disciple. I knew many people who read the Gospels: he lived in them. I knew many who were trusting the Lord: Mr Matheson walked with him. Like Paul with the believers in Thessalonica, my friend could say, 'We loved you so much that we were delighted to share with you not only the gospel of God but our lives as well, because you had become so dear to us' (1 Thessalonians 2:8).

Constant watchfulness

'Always be on the look-out for prepared souls' was the very wise counsel of H. W Funnell of the China Inland Mission in my student days. Those words from the lips of this unassuming man of God have been a great help to me ever since. It is for God to make the opportunity: it is for us to take it. We should not be surprised that the Son of God said in John 6:44, 'No-one can come to me unless the Father who sent me draws him.' May our heavenly Father give us eyes to see, a heart to feel and a tongue ready to speak his truth, that 'word in season'. May he also give us the sense to see when a little practical help will open the way for spiritual help. Not that practical help is always the right key to open the door for direct evangelising. We must learn by experience when this is so.

Perseverance

We may have to face many disappointments in the Lord's service. He himself used a blind man who needed a second touch as a visual aid to let his closest disciples know that they were very slow on the uptake. People we thought were beginning to seek the Lord may make it obvious that they have lost interest. What looked so encouraging may prove to be a fickle mirage. But we must not grow disheartened. Remember the parable of the sower: some seed did fall on good ground, though other did not.

We must encourage ourselves with the Scriptures and the remembrance of God's sovereignty in salvation. It is the work of the Holy Spirit to take the Word of God to those who have been chosen by God and to make them his children. But I want to put that Word into as many hands as I can, even though I am acutely aware that I cannot make one child of God. That work is in better hands than mine.

12
How should we give?

Dr Paul White, the Jungle Doctor, tells of two African lepers who were desperately eager to help the missionaries. Their hands were so eaten away with the leprosy that they were just bandaged stumps. For several weeks they worked in the deep saw-pit, sawing logs into boards for the extension of the bush hospital. When they had finished, each man was given his wages. The doctor noticed them dividing it into piles of silver. They explained that half was for the Lord.

'But that's too much. God only asks for a tenth.'

'But, Bwana,' one of them quickly replied, 'we love him far more than that.'

A pattern of giving
Giving like this illustrates the teaching which Paul sets out in 2 Corinthians 8 and 9, where we can without difficulty trace a pattern of Christian giving. The giving of the Corinthian Christians, as ours should be, was

Joyful (8:2)
In spite of the fierce testings and deep poverty of the Macedonian Christians, they had joyfully contributed to the relief of their needy fellow Christians in Jerusalem. This need had arisen because their previous source of help had been cut off since they had become Christians. The one

group of Christians helped the other, not from any ulterior motive but simply from an overflow of joy.

Sacrificial (8:3)

Paul praises them for giving not only according to their ability but beyond it. He would not advocate a Christian going into debt in order to give to the Lord's work, nor depriving his dependants of the necessities of life. But do we know what it means to go without some 'extra' we would very much like, in order that some other Christian may have what he or she really needs?

Voluntary (8:3)

They were not bullied into giving. They did not merely give because they were emotionally stirred by pictures of starving children. They gave willingly. If we really know and love the Lord, we too shall be willing to give for his sake.

Systematic and proportional

In Paul's first letter to the Corinthian Church, he had advocated systematic giving. It is not for the church or its leaders to tell us what to give. This is a matter between the Lord and ourselves. The allusion to 'each man' (9:7) emphasises our personal responsibility to decide how much and to whom we shall give. Paul only goes so far as to say that every Christian, every week, should put aside a gift 'as the Lord has prospered him' to be used for the work of the Lord (1 Corinthians 16:2 AV).

Some will find missionary boxes helpful. Some will give direct to societies. Some will use part of the amount for literature they give away personally. Each Christian needs to weigh up prayerfully what proportion of his giving should be to the local church he is in fellowship with. It is possible that the proportion may vary from time to time as needs may vary.

Determined (8:4)

On their own initiative the Macedonian Christians begged Paul to accept gifts they brought. They counted it a privilege and a favour to be allowed to share in this service to their fellow Christians. Do we look on Christian giving as a burden we must carry or as a privilege we may share?

Generous (9:7)

God loves a cheerful giver. Generous giving affords proof of our sincerity as Christians. 'Love must express itself in action, just as faith must issue in works' (R. V. G. Tasker).

Many Christians wish they had more to give and long to do more to meet the needs of fellow Christians, especially those in full-time Christian service. But God does not expect us to give what we don't possess! However little we possess, we can be generous, for generosity is in attitude as well as in action. He understands our financial position. Five pounds may be an exceedingly generous gift from one giver—and a very small gift from someone else. Our Lord rated the widow who cast into the temple treasury her day's wages as being more generous than any other giver that day, although many had cast in far larger amounts.

Hindrances to giving

Paul, in this portion of God's Word, also reminds us of common hindrances to Christian giving.

Unfulfilled promise (9:1-4)

Failure to continue what was well begun can mar our

Christian giving. Have we stopped giving what the Lord called us to give, what we are in a position to give, and what we said we would give? We are to plan thoughtfully what and how we are to give, and to act accordingly.

Meanness (9:6)

Christians should never be tight-fisted when it comes to Christian giving. A farmer who is generous with his seed will reap a better harvest than one who isn't. So a generous person will reap bountifully in his spiritual life.

Reluctance (9:7)

To give because we are cornered, or because we feel forced to give, or merely to get our names on some subscription list, is not true Christian giving.

Outworkings of Christian giving

Finally, let us look at some of the outworkings of Christian giving.

The maturing of Christian character (8:7; 9:8)

Christian giving forms an important part in Christian maturity. Faith in Christ, knowledge of his Word, earnestness in his service, all need to be rounded off by generosity. I have yet to meet a mature Christian who has not begun to exercise Christian stewardship.

The meeting of mutual need (8:13-15)

Christian giving is not designed to transfer the strain from one to another, but to share out the strain more evenly. Generous giving does not remain one-way traffic for long. Those who relieve the pressure on others may, at some time in their life, find their own abundance drying up in some economic crisis, and others coming to their aid. The New Testament does not teach that all Christians should have exactly the same material resources as each other. For the needs of all are not alike. Nor has everyone the same ability for handling money and property wisely. Responsibility varies with capacity.

Sharing in Christian service
All over the world there are Christians in full-time service for Christ, whose income would be two or three times greater if they had stayed at home in their professions or trades. Yet for Christ's sake they have surrendered this considerable extra amount for the work of the gospel. Equally for his sake, it is our responsibility to see that neither his work nor his servants suffer for lack of our gifts. (See Romans 15:27 and 1 Corinthians 9:14.)

Spiritual enrichment is the Lord's reward to all who fulfil this responsibility. Many of us will know Christians who have proved themselves to be good stewards, who can testify that the more they gave as the Lord prompted, the more he prospered them and gave them to go on giving. It is a glorious, not a vicious, circle!

The motive for Christian giving (8:9; 9:8,15)
Christ gave himself, nothing less, for us. We must give ourselves, nothing less, to him. And we must give ourselves before we give anything else (8:5). Nothing we can give can ever compare with God's unspeakable gift to us—the Lord Jesus Christ. He exchanged his heavenly wealth for human poverty, so that we might know the riches of his grace. And his grace is the mainspring of all genuine Christian giving.

He is able to make all grace—every aspect of his undeserved love—abound toward us, no matter how our

111

circumstances may change, 'so that in all things at all times, having all that [we] need, [we] will abound in every good work' (9:8).